Professions

Professions

100 spirit-awakening poems
by Dr. Jaerock Lee

URIM
BOOKS

Professions by Dr. Jaerock Lee
Published by Urim Books (Representative: Seongnam Vin)
73, Yeouidaebang-ro 22-gil, Dongjak-gu, Seoul, Korea
www.urimbooks.com

Unless otherwise noted, all Scripture quotations are taken from the Holy Bible, NEW AMERICAN STANDARD BIBLE, ®, Copyright © 1960, 1962, 1963, 1968, 1971, 1972, 1973, 1975, 1977, 1995 by The Lockman Foundation. Used by permission.

First Published in March 2015

Previously published in Korean in 2014 by Urim Books in Seoul, Korea

Edited by Dr. Geumsun Vin
Designed by Design Team of Urim Books
Printed by Prione Printing
For more information contact: urimbook@hotmail.com

Foreword

Once I was dreaming about bright future like any other young men. I was planning my life thinking I would go to a good college, study abroad, and become a great man. But unlike my dreams, in my twenties my life rushed downhill into the mire of despair.

Right after my marriage, sudden sickness struck me and ruined my whole body. I couldn't do anything as the head of the family. Instead I was only a burden to them. My brothers used to love me very much, but as my sicknesses were prolonged, they gradually kept their distance from me. I thoroughly realized the love among siblings is so meaningless. I also felt deep in my bones the heartbreaking pain of poverty.

But on one of those days while I was suffering in the swamp of despair, God came to me and met me. The moment I knelt before Him in a church, He healed all my diseases at once. Since then God has become everything in my life.

As I met God and began to feel His love, I was dying to know His heart and will more completely. Whenever I had time I prayed and I listened to sermons in every revival meeting I knew that was being held. I always sought to understand the will of God with the eagerness of a tree that stretches out its roots to a distance of scores of yards looking for water. This desperate heart of mine is well expressed in this book.

> My dear Father,
> I went up to the mountains and knelt before You
> In order to understand Your true will.
> This son of yours wants to spread Your deep love,
> And this son wants that
> Not so many people misunderstand You,
> But that they truly believe in You.

Eventually, God clearly let me know His endless heart

and will that is contained in the Bible. He also let me know the professions that God, the Lord, and the patriarchs of faith made from their hearts. I have compiled these professions of heart and published them into this book *'Professions'* in order to share these overwhelming emotions with many people.

The first part of the book has the professions of God, which is His heart towards mankind. It also has the professions that the first man Adam made and also those of the patriarchs of faith such as Enoch, Noah, Abraham, Jacob, Joseph, and Moses. We can feel the love of God the Father who created human beings with great hope, desiring to share love with them.

My heart is so vast,
Who could understand this heart?
Even though I would like to give,
There is nobody to receive.
Even though I would like to share it,
There is nobody to share it with.
There is nobody to understand
This vast, great, and deep heart of Mine.

And therefore, I will reveal My love
Through Those who will understand My heart

God created all the cells and organs of man with His
great love. He created man's eyes, ears, nose, mouth,
hands and feet, and all the internal organs with His best
effort, and then He breathed into his nostrils the breath
of life. Since that time, with His love He has been leading
all lives in the course of human cultivation.

I have made you people,
And therefore I take responsibility for you
And I guide you.
If you believe in Me and obey Me,
You will see My glory.
You will feel the love of the Father.
I am your Father who created you.

God has a great and vast heart that is more than able
to cover the whole universe, and He is full of love. But
because He is spirit, we cannot see Him with our eyes,
and some people do not feel His love. For this reason
God sent His only begotten Son Jesus. God proved and

confirmed His love to the people who were destined to fall into eternal death due to the sin of disobedience. He opened the way of salvation and glory for them.

The second part of the book is the professions of Jesus and the professions of John the Baptist, Peter, John, and Paul. The professions of Jesus are the professions that He made during His ministry on this earth.

Father,
The calming sound of the water on the shore
Lets me feel the gentle touch of Your hands.
This tranquility, the mild sound of the waters,
The faces of the beloved ones,
Through these
I deeply feel the heart of the Father who sent Me.

It was a profession that Jesus made to the Father, feeling the warm love of the Father while He was having a short rest at the shore of Galilee during His busy ministry. Jesus spent very busy days teaching the disciples, preaching the gospel, and showing signs. Sometimes He had to sleep on a boat; sometimes He had to share hardened bread with His disciples. And God the Father would have looked at this Jesus with such loving eyes.

Jesus did not think about Himself but only the souls even while He was going through cold, hunger, and many other sufferings. And this love of His is embedded in His professions. He was very passionate for the souls that were sin-stained for He knew about the beauty and happiness of Heaven so very well.

Right before the suffering of the cross began, He offered up a beautiful profession to the Father saying, "Now, the time has come for Me to fulfill the beautiful providence of the Father." He did not first think about the sacrifice He had to make, but He first prayed for the disciples who would remain, and remembering the disciple who would betray Him, He said, "His last image pierces My heart."

He went the way of sufferings with the hope that so many souls would receive life. Until the last moment on this earth, He prayed to the Father God for His beloved ones.

The third part of the book is mainly my professions. Several years ago, I was in Galilee on a pilgrimage together with church members. My heart was deeply moved when I felt each drop of water there contained the breath of Jesus transcending 2,000 years' of time.

This place that I am seeing is
The same place that the Lord was seeing...
My dear Lord, were You here?
Is this the place You passed by?
What did You think, and what did You speak of?

Trying to think of the ministry of the Lord, I made up my mind to have the love of the Lord to love the souls with all my life.

Only if I could, I'd like to give my eyes, my ears,
My hands, my arms, my breath,
And even my soul and everything for the souls...
I'd not want to give up even one,
There is not one of them that I do not love...
My heart is full of enabling love.

I earnestly hope that the seeds of love and faith that the Lord had scattered with all His life should produce beautiful fruits. I pray that all the readers will feel the billows of God's love and their hearts will be filled with loving emotions.

February 2014,

Jaerock Lee

Contents

Foreword

Chapter 1
My Dear Father

Chapter 2

The Lord My Bridegroom

Chapter 3
Father, Lord, Me

Chapter 1

My Dear Father

I will show My love

My heart is so vast,
And who would understand this heart?
Even though I would like to give,
There is nobody to receive.
Even though I would like to share it,
There is nobody to share it with.

There is nobody to understand
This vast, great, and deep heart of Mine.
And therefore, I will reveal My love
Through Those who will understand My heart.

I am Who I am,
But because of My heart and My love
I will put limitations on Myself.

My heart that is decided today
Will later speak of My space, heart, and love,
And I will rejoice
Because of this decision I have made.

The heart of the original God who came to
exist as the Trinity after planning for human
cultivation to gain true children with whom
He could share true love

I am your Father who created you

I have made you people,
And therefore I take responsibility for you
And I guide you.

If you believe in Me and obey Me,
You will see My glory.
You will feel the love of the Father.
I am your Father who created you.

I am Your Father who created you.

The providence of God,
who created human beings and has been
cultivating them, taking the responsibility for
them and leading them

Will these men truly understand
My heart?

My long-standing hope and desire
Is contained in this man.
Through all these beautiful things that I am doing,
I wish all My hopes and plans
Will be completely fulfilled…

My powerful hands
Touch each part to make organs
And all that is in the body.
Through this man who is made beautifully,
I will be glorified.

Through the son and the other son
My beauty, compassion, meekness,
Fullness of love, and almightiness will be proclaimed.

I make this mouth,
I make the lips, ears, and hands,
Feet and all that is in the body beautifully.

Through this birth of man now,
My long-standing hopes and wishes will
Be made true.

Will this man truly understand My heart?
Will he understand My heart?
Will he understand this love of the Father
Who is making each cell, organ,
And every part of his body?

My long-lasting desire
Created this man,
And all things will last until latter days for My glory.

The profession of God's heart that He made
when He was molding the first man Adam
with great expectations and love,
and with all His best efforts

You gave me the authority over all created things…

Father,
The sound of the breeze that touches my ears
Bears Your gentle voice,
And I feel the Your breath from the breeze.

In the flow of the winds
Is embedded Your will
That runs all things in the universe.
I feel the touch of Your hands that rule over all things.

When You created each of these things,
You put Your heart in them to reveal Yourself.
I can feel Your breath in the breaths
Of the mountains and streams, plants and grass.

I did not see with my own eyes
When You were creating all things in the universe.
But I feel Your warm hands, and I feel Your greatness
Through all the things that You,
Who are almighty, have created.

Father,
You gave birth to me
To make me joy in Your eyes and a fruit of Your work.

This son of Yours has received Your love
And has been set high above all things by Your grace.
Therefore, Father, receive the praise and glory
Through the lips of this son.

You created all these things in the beginning,
You spread Your love in them,
And You put Your love in each of them.
You created me in a way
That this son can praise Your greatness.

Father, with Your power
You created me.
You gave me the authority to subdue everything.

For this reason, this son of Yours,
Along with many others,

Is constructing this structure to honor You,
And to honor the authority You gave me.

I have built this structure
To show the greatness of the Triune God
That is revealed in all things of the universe,
And to show the whole heart of the Father.
Therefore, Father, accept it.

This beautiful structure
Becomes comfort in the heart of the Father,
And the authority and dignity of this son
Who has built it
Is lifted high, as well.

Father, You gave birth to this son of Yours,
And You gave me the power to build this structure.
Therefore, I'd like it to be Your joy,
And I'd like it to be comfort to You.

Father,
Though this is merely a tiny structure in Your eyes,
I desire that through this
Your name will be further glorified.

As the power that You've given me is revealed here,
All created things kneel before
This son of Yours to whom You gave birth.
The name of this son is also glorified.

Father, thank You.
Father, receive all the glory.
Receive all the glory through this son.
Father, I only want to become joy and comfort to You.

Adam's profession offered to the Father God
after he completed the structure that reveals
God's glory on this earth while Adam was still
living in the Garden of Eden.

The Father will be pleased

It is beautiful!
Its brilliance does not compare
With anything of this earth.

It is majestic!
Its majesty reveals the majesty of the Father.

The colors that it reflects at dusk
Express the beauty of the Father.
He will be pleased to see it.

On this land that is so quiet as if there was nothing,
The majesty of the Father is revealed.
The Father's will in letting me rule over this place
Is finally shining.

Adam's profession offered to God
after he completed the three structures
that represent God the Trinity.

Was I so foolish?

What happened?
What have I done?

I thought I could do anything at my will,
But I am miserable now.

The throng that was escorting me,
The Father's authority that I had,
Now they are all taken away from me
And this rough land feels heavy on me.

Why have done it?
Why have I forsaken the love of the Father?
How could I have been so foolish?
How will I live on this rough land?

Adam's lamenting profession he made
after he was driven out of the Garden of Eden
for eating from the tree of the knowledge of
good and evil.

I will take heed and be watchful

I stand on this earth humbled
And having seen better days.
How foolish is this?
How many days will I live here?
How many days will I have to count living a life here?
I am so insignificant and so wretched.

It is so completely different,
From the times when I came down to this first heaven
While living in the second heaven.
Now as I look at the things here
– the land, the environment, and the animals –
They are not the same as those that I used to see.

I am so afraid and troubled because of this.
Because I committed a sin this is what was decided.
And thus I will have to do my best in this life here.

I will organize my thoughts and long for heaven,
But how long will I have to live this life
Handed out by the Father?

I will count each day of my life until it ends here,
To take heed and be watchful
Concerning all the things I have done.

For the things that happened to this earth
That are because of me,
I will spend each day of my life,
With an apologetic and penitent heart
And truly expiating attitude,
For all the things that I see
That are now so desolate and so lonesome.

It feels like I can touch heaven,
But I can't. It is so, so far away.
How lamentable and so regrettable!
But I will consider this situation fortunate
Because I have received another life from the Father.

I am afraid and tremble before this new life,
But I have no choice but to live this life given to me.
When my life ends here on this earth

I will be able to meet the Father.
I will be able to see Him again.

Adam's profession made with a repenting heart for his foolishness, spending many days with tears after he had committed sin and had been driven out to this earth.

This hour feels like a dream

It feels like but a short ago,
When I was so worried about
How I was going to live here.
But already it's almost time for me to go.

I did not know how to live,
But the Father poured His grace down on me.

As He had done then,
The Father again gave me
The hope, courage, and strength to live.

I was able to eat and not starve,
I had a beloved family,
And I learned the meaning of tears.
I learned the meaning of joy,
And the meaning of happiness.
For these reasons life on this earth has not been
So sorrowful or painful.

The Father is calling me at this hour,

And it seems like a dream
That I am going to that place.

I will once again confess my foolishness to the Father.
Again I will ask Him for forgiveness,
For His heart was broken because of me,
And then I will offer Him all my thanks.

Having gained hope for Heaven after he had
gone through the human cultivation on this
earth, this is the profession Adam made just
before he breathed his last on this earth.

What kind of person is He?

There have been many teachings
That I received from my ancestors
But, in this hour being by myself,
Seeing the trees and everything here
That spreads out before me,
Once again, I think about who created these things,
And who created this vast world.

He is in me.
He is the One who created all these beautiful things.
He is the One who created the grandfather
Of my grandfather, and his grandfathers.

He created this world that spreads out endlessly.
He let me be here today,
For He has consideration for men and loves them.
He is my Father.
I think of Him.

When I am alone,
While looking up into the sky

I imagine the face of the Father.
When I comfortably relax and step on this ground,
My heart is touched because I feel
The providence and greatness of the Father.

Based on the things I learned from my fathers,
As I feel the 'Father'
And as I open my mouth and praise Him,
I love Him more and more day by day,
And my longing for Him gets deeper and deeper.

The more I think of what kind of person He is,
Rather than the teachings I received from my fathers,
The greater my longing for Him becomes.
The more this longing of mine sinks in,
The more deeply ingrained into my heart it becomes.

What does His face look like?
What kind of smile does He have?
Who is He that He sent us here
To hear the breath of this earth,

And to feel the sky and sense the stars in the sky?
I can feel His breath from the air that I breathe in…

My Father lets me open my mouth to praise Him.
But who is He who lets me open my mouth
And profess what I have come to realize?
Do you know just who and what He is?

How can I meet Him who dwells in such a vast space?
How can I engrave Him in my heart
while living my life?
I imagine my Father and again I imagine Him,
With so much longing that is etched deep in my heart.
What kind of person is He?

Adam's seventh generation Enoch's
profession made with longing for the Father
God, just before he received the blessing of
walking with God.

Seeing just a blade of grass

All these things that the Father has created,
They are beautiful, so delightful.

I feel the heart of the Father
Even in just a blade of grass.

The word of the Father is in me,
And I take delight in
Conversing with the Father all the time.

It is my joy
To offer myself to the Father,
And to praise Him at different times.

Rather than meeting and speaking with people,
I find greater joy,
In seeing the world that He created,
And professing my heart to the Father alone.

I long for the place where the Father is.

In seeing just a single blade of grass and
feeling the love of God from the goodness of
his heart, Enoch made this profession before
he was taken up to Heaven.

The greatest joy of this son

Father,
You have loved this son so much,
And now You have brought me
Into this beautiful place
To add even more to my joy.

The love You have given me
Is already impossible to number,
And yet you still are giving me this vast and fair place.

The greatest joy of this son,
Is that I can be with You all the time,
And upon that joy You add Your love.

After being taken up to Heaven and
entering into New Jerusalem, this is Enoch's
profession made with his love and joy upon
seeing his heavenly home that was made
exactly according to his preferences.

Father, what should I do?

Father,
Seeing this Ark as it is being built,
I feel the prominence of the day that is coming.
But, this Ark being built,
Rather than becoming a source of joy to me,
Instead it makes me feel anxious
And desperately pitiful distress.

I have not been lazy,
And I have been preparing everything
Relying on the word of the Father.
I have been faithful day and night in all aspects.
But as each of the things is prepared
And each of them is completed,
Due to the impending significance of that day,
There is only desperate pity.

In the commands that the Father has given me,
In order to fully keep them all,
I have kept each in mind and completed each of them.
And now the shape of the Ark is being revealed,

And since it has been prepared precisely
As commanded,
When I see the people of this world,
I only feel extreme pity for them.

This is because I know the heart of the Father.
Even though I spread the news to them,
They do not listen,
Even though I speak to them they cannot hear.

They have the ears but cannot hear;
They have the eyes but cannot see.
I feel sorry for them for they just pass the time
Without knowing where they came from
And where they are going.

Now according to the Father's command,
I and my family will go into this Ark,
And all other things that have been appointed
By the Father will go in there, too.
But when I think,

'What will become of those people in the world?'
My compassion for them only deepens.
But even though I have pity for them,
How can my heart be like the heart of the Father,
And how can I understand it?

Relying on the word of the Father,
I can forsake everything that I have.
Therefore, even though I do not understand
The heart of the Father completely,
I sense the reason
Why the Father ordered me to build the Ark
And to prepare and accomplish everything
One step at a time.

But my heart is so desperate
Because I feel the day is so near.
And Father, please understand my heart,
That is so desperate for those people.

Father, what should I do?

They do not know the Father.
Even though they see, they cannot see.
Even though they hear, they cannot hear.
In the plan of the Father
All these things are being revealed,
But they do not feel anything.
How can I make them turn away?

Father,
This son of Yours will do my best
Until the day You command me,
For all things will be done in Your will.

Always lead me and guide me
So that this son will not make a mistake
In accomplishing everything precisely
In accordance with Your will.

Noah's profession offered to God while he
was building the ark, seeing the people who
did not listen to him when he preached the
impending punishment of the flood.

I give thanks to my Father.

My Father, my Father,
My Father, You guide my whole life.
I received Your guidance,
And I was in Your love during all the days of my life.

My Father, my Father,
I give You thanks,
For letting me live by Your will only.

I give thanks to You, my Father,
For You let me have the eyes of faith
And the heart of obedience,
To make my life honorable.

When You wanted something,
You let me understand it and obey You.
Thank You for guiding me so I could be blameless.

Abraham's profession of thanksgiving offered
to the Father God some time after he served
the men of God (Genesis 18).

Father, receive glory greatly!

While I have life and I breathe,
Father God, You have guided me,
In Your providence and will,
And as I sum up everything before my death,
You touch my heart
And allow for me to feel happiness in my heart.
You let me take this way with joy and thanksgiving.
Father, I give you all thanks and glory.

I have been blessed in my life,
Because, Father, you loved me and guided me.
I have been full and I have lacked nothing,
As I dwelt in Your love.

Even up until this moment facing my death,
You move my heart and I am embraced
As You draw me to Your bosom.
I give You thanks and glory.

In Your sight, Father,
I tried to show perfect faith,

But sometimes I used my own thoughts.
But Father, because You love me,
You opened all the ways for me.
You guided me and You molded me in every way.

Father, You refine me to perfect me,
And my thanks for You has been stored up
So that when I see all things,
I do not see them with the eyes of the actualities,
But I see them with the eyes of the Father.
Father, I give You thanks
For guiding me to have such a heart.

And today, I have with me this wealth,
This honor, this fame,
And this glory of the Father,
So that I am praised by many,
And my son gives me joy, and I give You thanks.
I have not had any illness during my entire life,
I have not had any hardship in my life.

I give You thanks
For there was no hardship or suffering
In my body or in any other aspect.
And I give thanks
For now I see the providence of God
That I will be at the bosom of the Father
After I breathe my last.

Father,
I give You thanks that I am filled with
Thanksgiving, joy and delight facing my death.

And now,
Eerything is in accordance with Your providence.
Father,
Even though I lay down all these physical things
I believe that all Your plans
Will be fulfilled completely
In the providence of the Father.
And I believe that Your providence through this son
Will be completely fulfilled.

Father, I give You thanks.
I give You thanks that I go to be before You
And I will be so peacefully at Your bosom.

Life on this earth is utterly meaningless,
But Father, You made it
So my life has not been meaningless.
You made it so precious and worthy,
So that as I face my death,
I can be at Your bosom
Being full of joy, thanksgiving, and delight.
And for this, Father, I give You thanks.

Everything is in Your hands, Father,
And Father, receive glory greatly,
Through all these things.

Abraham's profession of thanksgiving offered
just before his death as he was thinking of the
Father whom he would soon see.

Grace and blessings given to me

My God,
Throughout my life, I wanted to do everything
The way that I saw fitting;
In the way I wanted to live
And in the way I desired for things to be
And I wanted to have,
And I wanted to achieve all these things on my own.

But in the end I felt and realized
That it was wrong after all.
Truly, all my thoughts,
All the things that were in my heart,
All my greed and desire to take things,
Were revealed before God completely
So that I could come forth clean,
So that I could rid myself of all those desires
So that I could I understand
What God's will is and what is true.

Living this kind of life I had been living,
It's not that I had no regrets at all

At each moment of my life,
But now I thank You, God,
That in Your precious intervention,
You changed me and guided me,
And now You let me beget these many children,
And these children receive blessings of God.
I want all of them to dwell
In the providence of salvation of God,
And I want them to go their way
In the will of God.

When I was truly foolish,
I had willingness to go against the will of the Father,
I had my own will to do the things my own way,
And I wanted to achieve with my own wisdom.
But I have realized that all those things were nothing.

My God,
As I met God and as I learned about God in my heart
In the ways of trials,
I hope all those who have come by me

Will keep the heart of God in their minds,
And remember it,
So that they will fulfill the works of God.
Although there were explosive things,
Hardships, and difficulties
While living my life as given here,
The grace and blessings
That You have given me, Father,
Are so great, how can I give You thanks enough!

Truly, my God,
And God of my father, and God of my grandfather,
My beloved God, I give You thanks
For changing me to be who I am now
And to be with You.

Now, accept me.
And, my God, let me be where You are
So that my heart will be in peaceful comfort.
I believe that You will fulfill
Your will and providence in me,

And that You will achieve what You have promised
Through the ones that remain.

I give You thanks,
That You loved me and let me be in Your grace.
I give thanks before God,
That now all the tears, pain of the heart, sorrow,
Parting with my beloved one,
And all other things buried in my heart
Come as perfect comfort in my heart in God.

I give thanks,
That through all these things that happened to me
You let me see all things in the providence of God,
Even until this moment that I am closing my eyes.

My God,
I give You thanks for guiding my way.
I give You thanks for giving me honor and happiness
Until today with Your love.
I give thanks for letting me

Be in the grace of God.

Jacob's profession of thanksgiving made just
before his death, for God's grace in changing
him

I believe the providence of God will be fulfilled

My beloved God,
I give You thanks my God,
For even in the indiscretions of my youth
You considered me and guided me,
You led me into the truth.

Everything in my life has been peaceful
And all things have been prosperous.
It's been by the grace of the Father.
You considered a lowly person like me
And led me to be perfected.
You brought many people
To kneel before the name of the LORD God.
You let me fulfill the providence of God.
My God, I give You thanks.

I give thanks that in all my life
There was nothing lacking and no shortage,
Everything was abundant.
The grace of God was overflowing,
And the blessings and grace given by God

Were so great.
My God I offer You my thanks.

I close my eyes now,
However, in all things that remain,
Let God's will and providence be done.
Let the beam of grace always shine on everyone
So that they will not forget the grace of God.
Give many people more understanding in their hearts
That they should never forget God's grace,
And lead them in all their ways.

I have been here because God has been here.
I give You thanks that,
In the grace and blessing of God,
I have been made honorable
And I have made God known to many people.

There was a flood of evidence that God loved me
And God's love has been overwhelming to me.
I give You thanks that You accomplished

So many things through me,
You have reaped such great fruit,
And You were delighted.

I give You thanks
That although I was truly nothing
And I could not do anything,
You still considered me and loved me.
You guided my way,
So that I had a long life and received blessings.
Until this moment I end my life on this earth,
For me all things have been prosperous.
Thank You my God.

Now, for all the things that will take place later,
I believe everything will be done
In Your providence and will, my God.
Let Your grace overflow from this place,
And let Your grace not stop for the people of God.

I give You thanks.

I give You thanks for loving me.
I give You thanks for giving me grace.
I give You thanks for giving me all this honor.
I give You thanks
That I can close my eyes in that honor.
I give You thanks.

I commit everything into God's hands,
And I peacefully go to His bosom,
And therefore, hold this son of God,
Your beloved and pleasing son in Your bosom,
And take delight in him.

Profession of Joseph, who gave glory to God
greatly being the prime minister of Egypt,
made just before his death giving thanks for
God's love and asking Him to take care of
His people.

God who personally called me

The One who is in heaven,
God!

I was foolish,
And I did not know about You.
But now, just by seeing the sunset,
I believe in the existence of the Almighty God.

Even though I intend to have anything,
I can't have it.
Even though I try to gain anything,
I cannot gain it.
Thus, I am so meaningless that I am nothing.
However, I believe in my heart
That God exists and He loves me.
I believe that He is the One
Who is personally calling me.

Moses' profession made after he realized
about the living God during his life in the
desert for forty years which he lived after
he left the life in the palace being a son of a
princess of Egypt

They are so precious to me

My Father,
My love and longing for You
Is increasing day by day.

No matter what hindrance blocking the way,
It can't stop the hand of the Father.
And there is nothing that can stop
My love for the Father
That grows moment by moment.

I hope that each soul
Will be in the hands of the Father,
And will not commit sins with their hands or lips,
But will come forth as the kind of people
Whom the Father wants.

Father, because You molded them and created them,
Each of these souls is so precious to me.
Let them not forget the grace of the Father.
Keep their lips so that they will not commit sins.
Let them not enrage the Father

With their weak faith,
But add more grace so that
They will be pleasing in Your sight.

I am only Yours, Father.

Moses' profession that he made with the
desire for the souls not to commit sins after
he had been renewed as the leader that God
wanted through the forty years of trials in the
desert.

Finishing the duty given by the Father

Father,
The land that You blessed
Is such a fertile and beautiful land.

I cannot look at it closely,
But I know it's a good place
Where I can feel the heart of the Father.

I remember the time You were with me,
While I was leading these people
For a many, many days.
You truly did many works, leading them with patience.

When I first began the duty that You gave me,
I was lacking in so many ways.

Even now, before You, Father,
I am such a little one, but as my time is now ready
I commit to You all the things that are to be done
In the days that are to come.

The Father's majestic Glory
Is known around here,
Your majestic Glory that has been stored up,
I want it to continue more greatly with these people.

Through this prayer,
Which is the last thing I can give to these people,
As You did for me with Your heart,
Father, I want Your grace to overflow
Onto these people, as well.

Moses' profession given to the Father God
watching the Canaan Land, the land flowing
with milk and honey, after finishing his duty

I am starting this work...

I am starting…
For the tears of My Son
To become precious to them,
For this evil generation shouting
To show My love to them,
To My Son who understands the depth of My heart,
I am harshly starting this work…

Because I know
That My beloved Son will lead them to understand
That My heart is such deep love,
I am starting this work.

Until I, the LORD God Almighty,
Become their Father,
I will not stop this work.

The profession of God the Father who was
beginning to do the work that would make so
many people His true children through His
beloved Son.

Have you seen those tears?

Have you seen those tears,
Those uncontrollable tears
That flow down so endlessly?

My son knows that it is painful
For Me to see My son's face with My eyes,
And it is the grace given to them,
And because My son knows it,
He takes his way only with thanksgiving,
And to Me this is all the more painful.

People do not know Me because of their evil,
But in order to let them know about Me,
I put a great burden on My beloved son.
The result is fruit at cost of My tears of love
and those of My beloved son.

Just a little more, just a little more…
Go forward, go forward…
I am shouting towards My son
in the depths of My heart.

> Encouraging profession that the Father God
> made, seeing His beloved son pray with
> mournful tears to fulfill the providence of the
> end time.

The Father wants them to enter Heaven

I established this altar
Because I love you.
I showed you many ways of love
That you could not possibly fathom.

If you understand the heart of the Father,
Who has given you the shepherd to lead you
In a way as if you were seeing Me,
You would know what great grace it is
That you can breathe,
You can hear him, and you can talk to him.

I am much greater, wider, and more full of love…
Way more than you think.

I want everyone to come into
This place that I prepared.
I am the faithful One
Who helps you to have the qualifications.
I do not want to forsake you,
But I want you to reach salvation; I am your Father.

I am the One who enabled you to call me Father.
I am the One who prepared salvation.
I am the One who will lead you to Heaven.
I am the One who gave you your shepherd.

I want you to catch this chance of love,
And come forth as glorious fruits of your shepherd.

Loving profession of the Father God
who wants all believers to be saved and
to enter the city of New Jerusalem.

This place that I prepared

The grand plan of human cultivation
Is in My heart fully.
And my love for this plan is revealed
Through sacrifice.

Who would know
The love in My heart?
My plan is so great
That if one does not understand My original heart,
He would not be able to obey Me
And accept such great sacrifice.

My sons…
I want the souls to know My loving sacrifice for them,
The sorrows in My heart,
The goodness in My heart,
And the love in My heart…

The love in My heart will become tears
And fully bear the fruit of this grand plan of Mine.
My people…

My children…
May My name shine beautifully on this land.

In this place I prepared, My glory will shine.

I am the LORD God,
Your Father,
Who has given you everything for you.

The loving profession of the Father God
who has given us everything to lead each soul
to become His true children.

Chapter 2

The Lord My Bridegroom

Father, wait just a little longer.

The will of the Father,
His love…
For Me to leave the Father
Is such unbearable sorrow for Me.

However, it is also
Another way of expressing My love for the Father,
And it is going to be only for a little while.

As the beauty of this place is not comparable
With that of the earth,
This love that is in My heart
Has the measure that
These souls cannot even count.

The heart of the Father who is sending Me,
The great love of My Father,
The day this love is revealed before their eyes,

That is the reason why the Father is sending Me
Until I walk this way again

With the Father,
This short while
For Me will be such tremendous waiting.

Father,
I am fully ready.
I will go and come back, so wait just for a little while.
Your love will shine beautifully.

Jesus' profession to the Father when He was
ready to come down to this earth forsaking
the heavenly throne, in order to fulfill the
duty of the Savior.

Father, are You watching?

As if no one else exists,
This place is so calm and quiet.

The things that are seen,
The things that are seen in My eyes are but this sterile land.
Yet My heart is full of love.

Even in this place,
The love of the Father fills My heart fully.
The circumstances are different,
But My heart is the same.

Father, are you watching
This place?
With the eyes of the Father,
I am looking at this place.

This Son of Yours knows very well
How the Father created this earth
And how much You love the souls.
Even now I eagerly desire to be with You,

But this place is in such desperate need
Of the love of the Father for the souls
And the love of this Son.

Father!
Being hungry, and being tired,
And this exhaustion
I feel in this completely different space,
Make Me look like all the other fleshly people,
But let My heart be in the space of the Father.

This environment that is seen in My eyes,
Father, are You also seeing it?
Now, I will fulfill everything.

The profession of Jesus offered to the Father
God during His forty-day fast, which He did
to fulfill the duty of the Savior on this earth.

I see that You stand Me before Satan

Father,
This Son of Yours feels so thoroughly
What kind of space this is.

The things that are seen in My eyes,
And all the things that My body feels,
This space in which I am staying,

The limitations of this physical space,
All these things that I feel
Because I have a physical body,
I have not felt them before.

Only now I feel very deeply,
Why I was sent by You
To this place.

So many things were given to Me,
And I give You thanks for letting Me know
How I am supposed to use these many things,
And how I am supposed to achieve the goals.

Today, I see that You let me feel this space
So thoroughly, and that You stand Me
In front of Satan.

I feel the space of the Father
Who has stood Me
Before those beings that are nothing.

Profession of Jesus offered to the Father God
when He was led into the wilderness by the
Holy Spirit and fasted for forty days before
His public ministry began.

The one who prepares the way of the Lord

Father,
I give You thanks,
That You loved me,
That You let me receive the Lord
Who came here,
And that You let me see Him
Before my life is ended.

I give You thanks,
That You loved this man despite shortcomings,
That You let me receive
The precious Son of the Father,
And that You gave me the grace
To prepare the way for Him.

I was born an ordinary man,
But You let me reveal the glory of the Father.
You let me receive the Savior,
Of whom nobody is worthy.
You let me receive Your love,
Giving me the reward

With which nothing else can compare.
It is not something anyone can have
Just by longing for it.
I take this way with joy,
For I am able to complete everything,
Committing my life to the Father.

Now, I wish to be in Your bosom
In peace.

Profession of John the Baptist
offered to the Father God after completing his
duty to prepare the way for Jesus who came
as the Savior and just before his martyrdom.

Father, I give thanks

Father,
At this moment, shedding my tears,
I give thanks to You, Father.
I give thanks
That although there is one who will forsake Me,
There are others who will preach for Me as well.

There are ones who will suffer with Me,
And there are those who will give glory
To the Father through Me.

Father, this Son of Yours
Is not suffering alone, but the Father is with Me.
Even though it is full of hardships
To give My body for the souls and for the Father,
I still give thanks,
For there are those who know Me.

Just as I know the Father,
There are ones who know Me, too.
Father, thank You!

Father, thank You!

I have been with You Father
And I dwelt in Your glorious bosom
Since before the ages.
But, You sent Me for the souls,
And You know that now I am cold,
I hunger, and there are many sufferings.

Therefore, Father, at this moment,
I give thanks
That You let Me shed My tears of love
For the Father and for the souls.

Prayer of Jesus offered one night when it was
raining and cold: Jesus used to preach all day
and pray habitually at night.

To My Father

Abba, Father,
Whom I miss so deeply and so dearly

The air of this early morning
Enters into the depths of My heart as longing,
Like the voice of the Father.

The calming sound of the ripples
Refreshes My ears,
And it gives Me a moment's rest.

Just by thinking about You, Father,
I am happy, and I can have a smile on My lips.

Father, I go to different places today,
Where many people are waiting…
Yet You gave Me men of the Father besides Me,
And they help Me, and they give Me strength.
Father…
Father…
Whom I yearn to see…

After this day passes,
A day's work of the Father will be done,
And the day to see the Father is nearer.
Therefore, today also, I go towards the Father.

Jesus' profession offered to the
Father God sitting at the shore of Galilee, at
daybreak.

Watching the Galilee

Father,
Galilee has calmed down,
And its quietness soaks into the depth of My heart.

The lives of the souls on this earth
Truly look rough.

I wish they fully had
The beauty in the heart given by the Father...

And yet, Father,
Though I love this calmness of the seashore,
As I am sitting on this shore of Galilee,
And I think of the Father.

The gentle sounds of this silent shore
Feel like the touch of Your hands.

Father,
After I leave,
Many things will happen on this earth,

But I hope many of the people
Will feel that everything is the love of the Father.

Father,
I can hear the voice,
The voice of the beloved one of the Father,
The earnest and desperate cry to the Father,
The cry,
For the souls of this earth,
I can hear it in My ears.

While watching the seashore of Galilee,
I feel comfort
As if I were sitting in silence
On the seashore of Heaven.

The conversation I have with the Father
At this solitude and tranquil place
Moves My heart,
And it becomes the great heart of the Father
Who cannot help but love this earth.

I leave the beloved ones
On this earth,
And I hope Your eyes
Will be upon them always.

Through the stillness,
The sound of gentle ripples,
The faces of the beloved ones,
I feel deeply,
The heart of the Father who sent Me here.

Jesus' profession made sitting in the
boat looking up to the sky on the shores of
Galilee.

There is love of the Father and Heaven

Whew, the foolishness of the souls!
Why would they not understand
The heart of the Father?

Visible things are not everything,
How much more will they fall?
There is love of the Father and Heaven,
And how much further will they go?

If my heart is aching so,
How much more is the heart of the Father?
If they know My heart just a little bit,
They would know the power manifested before them
Is not trivial. What foolishness!

I want them to remember
This earnestness of My heart
With which I preach, and preach again.

Whew, Father, My Father,
I look up to the sky, wishing to see You.

Jesus' profession thinking of the
love of the Father, being heart-broken by
the foolishness of the people, while He was
preaching the gospel of the kingdom of heaven

Please hold them

Abba Father,
You sent this Son of Yours to this place
According to Your plan,
And the time that You destined has come.

I think of the days
During which I stayed with the disciples
In order to fulfill the providence of the Father.
Going from one place to another,
I spread the gospel
And I proclaimed the will of the Father.

But I am troubled
Because of the things that will be done
After I am gone.
All these things concern Me
And cause Me to agonize over them.
And therefore, I hope You will accept
The heart of this Son now praying.

I know it is such great honor to Me

To take the cross.
I know very well how much power of love
It will show to many people.
However,
The days I spent with the souls
In this physical space
To fulfill the will of the Father
Become tears in My eyes now.

Father,
Give strength to the weak disciples.
I know You will lead them,
And I know about the grace
That will come upon them
After I am gone.

For Me to be crucified
Is what is supposed to be done
For the glory of the Father,
So what is the reason why
All the things that happened in My public ministry

Come to me as agony
And fill My heart fully?

I realize that the heart I have being on this earth
Is very different
From the heart that I had in Heaven.
Many things concern Me and worry Me.

Father,
Please hold them.
Let all the things that You planned
Be achieved completely in You.

And receive glory greatly
Through the things that will be done
Through this Son.

Jesus' prayer offered at Gethsemane
thinking of the past just before the suffering
of the cross

Let him receive the Father's compassion

As for that son who is weeping and wailing so terribly,
Let him receive the Father's compassion.

I am thankful that what he realized in his heart
Will lead him in the way he is supposed to go.

When I said, "Get behind Me, Satan!"
He did not resent it,
But he tried to understand My will in his heart.
Therefore, Father, remember what he did.

Jesus' prayer offered to the Father
God committing Peter to the hands of God
knowing he would spend his days weeping
after he denied Jesus

Better had he not been born...

This preposterous act that he is committing
Will be unbearable for him,
And, I wish he had not been born...

His last image
Pierces My heart.

Jesus' profession offered with the
desire for Judas Iscariot to turn back, knowing
he would betray and sell Him out.

Let them not forget

My time has come.
The day to see the Father is near.
It means I have to leave them here.
Let them remember and keep in mind
The things I told them again and again.

With my concerns I commit them
Into the hands of the Father,
And now I feel much more relieved.
But there are so many things
That they will have to go through…

Father,
Tears roll down My face,
For I know of the sorrow
They will have after I am gone.

Let My beloved ones,
Not forget the times they had with Me
And the understanding they had gained.
Let them not forget

My earnest heart and My love for them.

Jesus' prayer offered to the Father God
thinking of His beloved souls whom He
would have to leave on this earth just before
the sufferings of the cross.

76 Professions

Time for the providence
to be fulfilled...

Father,
I remember the day when You first sent Me.

It was the day to say farewell to the Father,
And it was the beginning of My ministry.

Since then, this Son of Yours
Has been showing for many years
The heart of the Father
To the souls on this earth.

Sometimes tears rolled down on My face,
Sometimes smiles surrounded My lips,
Sometimes I became soaked
Just thinking about the Father.

In Your providence, You let me meet
Those whom I had to meet,
And I have done the things that You allowed.
I did all My best to fulfill Your will
During the days given to Me.

Now, the time is coming
To fulfill the beautiful providence of the Father.

I am trembling
Thinking of the time I had with these people,
Of those who will mourn for Me,
Of the Father who will be hurting
Because I will be hung.

Father, do not grieve,
For You will see Me soon and My glory is great.

Thinking of those who will remain,
You will give Your love to them,
And for this reason I am comforted.

My Father.

Jesus' profession made before the crucifixion,
thinking of the Father God who would feel
heart-broken and shed His tears.

The time will come for them to know love

Beloved Father,
My time has come,
And things are being done
According to Your will.

People are foolish and ignorant,
But in their heart that You created,
The time will come for them to know
The great love of the Father,
So do not be grieved.

I commit to You Father, once again,
These ones I love.

One loves Me,
But lacks in understanding.
Another has a fragile heart and has many tears.
Another has weak faith and has many thoughts.
Another has an upright heart
Which can be easily broken.
They will each go the way they are supposed to take

With their love for Me.
For some it is the way of the martyr,
For others the way of joy,
And for still others they will go the ways
That the Father wants them to take.

Father,
Through the one You will send,
Your plan will be fulfilled.

There is another who in her love for Me
Will live her life in tears.
Father, remember her.

Jesus' prayer after being arrested
to fulfill the providence of the cross that
was offered when He was imprisoned and
thinking of His disciples.

The love etched deep in My heart

I walk this way.
I cannot hear the words
That so many people around Me are saying to Me.
But why is it that
The sound of weeping of those women
Is heard so clearly in My ears?

The present sorrow will soon become glory.
Those tears will not be meaningless.
The Father will pay them back for those tears.

The tears they shed for Me are the tears of love.
The sorrow they have for Me
And their cries and their agony for Me
Are the love etched deep in My heart.

The scourging laid on Me,
And the heavy cross
That makes Me unable to feel My arms
Are the signs that I now have to leave this earth.
Father, My Father,

I am more than able to overcome,
So, neither sorrow nor grieve.

This Son of Yours will go to see You,
And it will be the glory of all glories.

Jesus' profession made when He
was going up Golgotha, while He was carrying
the wooden cross and shedding blood due to
flogging, thinking of the Father God and the souls

The reminiscence in My heart

Father, My Father,
You love all these things,
And You are perfect in Your Light.
The earth I stepped on
When I created it with You, Father,
And the people when they were first created
Are very different from those here now.

Father,
As I step on this land,
It is very different from
The time when I stepped on it with You
In the beginning.
The hearts of people are so different
From the heart that they had
When You created them.

Father,
Now I step on this land that is spoiled.
Father, as I now step on this spoiled land
I read the degenerate hearts of mankind.

But Father,
I have understood
Why You sent Me here,
And why You let me suffer with the things
That come from the heart of the corrupted men,
And why You let me come down here
From the glorious place
To let me feel these many things deep in My heart.

Father,
I am not afraid; I am absolutely fearless.
But I am truly heartbroken over the fact
That this earth was changed so very much
From the time I was here with You.

Father,
My heart is also aching
Because of the tainted hearts of the people.
But Father, I know that You will recover everything
In Your justice and the secret that has been hidden.

Father,
This is going to be only for a moment.
I take the cross with hope and joy, Father,
Because of the glory that You will give to Me,
And the ways of light
That You will open for these souls
After this is over.

Father,
It is not that this cross is heavy,
Nor is it that these thorns are painful,
But the tarnished earth
And the tarnished hearts of men
Which are very different
From the time I was here with You,
These are what weigh so heavily
On My heart so much.

But when all these things are over
After a short while,
You will open this way in Your permission

And in Your love,
And You will open up the light
And shine the beautiful light on Me,
So that I am more than able to go this way.

Father,
The ground I stepped on was gold,
The road I walked on was gold,
The scent of the flowers of this earth cannot begin
To compare that I used to smell,
The clothes I used to wear
Are completely different in their textures,
The place I used to live in was
Such a glorious place,
And I would like these people to know
About this beautiful and peaceful place.

Father,
I have thoroughly realized Your providence
Deep in My heart,
And why You begot Me,

Why You gave Me this duty,
And why You let Me come down to this place
To step on this tainted land,
And to read the degenerate hearts of men.
I praise You, Father,
For Your love, Your vastness,
And all the things that You do
Without a single error.

Father,
Do not turn Your face away from Me.
There is no shame before You Father,
For this burden that I am carrying.
Father, please do not feel sorry for Me.

I am overwhelmingly fulfilling this duty
That You have given,
So, Father, do not turn Your face away from Me,
But look at this Son.
Father, You are My last strength,
And You are My last power.

Father,
My heart is moved because,
After I take this burden and overcome everything,
You will turn Your face towards Me again,
And soon You will let Me participate
In the glory of the Father.

Father,
Do not feel sorry for My burden,
For this way I am taking,
Nor for all the sufferings that I am undergoing.
I am doing what I am supposed to do.
I am only going the way that is in Your providence.

My beloved Father,
People think that I am saying nothing,
And that I call Myself the king of the Jews.
But how will they understand or feel
The reminiscence that flows out from My heart,
The love towards You that flows out from My heart,

And the love towards these souls
That flows out from My heart?

Father,
Through the Holy Spirit whom You will give to them
After I am gone,
Many of them will come to understand and realize
The works that will take place later.
Therefore, Father, stop Your tears,
And do not turn Your face from Me.
Please do not feel sorry; please do not feel sorry.

As I look back and reminisce over many things,
I have so deeply grasped and perceived many things
About the work of human cultivation,
Giving birth to Me and separating Me,
And creating all these men.

Father,
All things are completed and perfectly done
To the point My tears become like a river

That wet My heart
And wet their hearts, too.
Father, therefore do not feel sorry. I love You.

Father,
I will think of this love with You
Until the moment I breathe My last on this earth,
And thus Father, do not feel sorry.
It is not that I cannot bear the weight
Of this cross that I am carrying.

Father,
I love You.
Until I shed all My blood
And I breathe My last on the cross,
Father, I recollect all the things
And look back on the hearts of all these people.

And so, Father, please do not feel sorry,
But receive glory through this Son.
Your providence and all Your plans

Will be fulfilled and completed fully and eternally.

Jesus' profession made while He
was going up Golgotha carrying the cross,
thinking about the providence of God.

I cannot live without You, Lord.

Lord, You are standing in front of Me,
And is it really You, Lord?
Lord, why would You just look at me from there?
I so dearly desire to be at Your bosom
And shed endless tears…
I earnestly hope to converse with You
About many things at Your bosom,
But I can only speak to You at a distance
For You would not allow it for me.

Lord, have You really resurrected?
You truly resurrected,
And I can see You with my eyes.
Lord, You live again!
When You were not here,
When I could not think that You would live again,
I never thought about my future,
As to how I would live in this world,
For surely I could not live without You.

Lord, You are standing before me,

Yet You are much more beautiful
Than You were before,
And therefore,
I look at You the way I am looking at You now.
You live again. Let me be at Your bosom once again!
Let me be at Your bosom!
Lord, I said I could not live without You.
But now, You are alive and in front of me,
So make a promise with me.
Promise me that You will hold me in Your bosom
And let me be where You will be.

You heard the words of this daughter
When You were on the cross.
As I said I could not live without You,
I could not think about what I would do
In a world where You do not exist.
Lord, my heart was pierced with great pain
At that moment.
You shed Your blood on the cross,
Yet You are in front of my eyes,

And You are so beautiful.

Lord, please promise me.
Let me be where You will be
So that I might serve You.
I cannot live without You.
Lord, now You live, so please promise me this.
Promise me that You will take me
And allow me to be next to You.
Lord, now do not leave me alone here.
Lord, Lord, I cannot live without You.

I have never thought of a life without You
Even for a moment.
For this reason,
When You breathed Your last
I did not know what to do.
I could not even plan how I was going to live.

I always said with my lips
That I could not live without You,

But now You live again
And have shown Yourself before me.
Lord, promise me! Take me into Your bosom,
And promise me that You would let me be
Where You will be.
That is my only wish and hope.

Lord, my only hope is that I will be
Where You will be
And serve You as I did on this earth.
Therefore, promise me that my wish will be fulfilled.

Mary Magdalene's profession made
when the Lord, who resurrected on the third
day, showed Himself to her for the first time

I will testify until the soles of my feet wear out

My love, my Lord, my beloved Lord,
He always gave me good things.
He loved me,
He is so precious.

I, Peter, deeply feel His love only now.
Many people rise up and speak for Him,
It is not something bad,
But I wish the name of the Lord
Were more gloriously mentioned.

There are many things to do.
A day's time is not enough to testify about the Lord
Whom I, Peter, witnessed,
And to testify about His love.

I, Peter, will testify the Lord
Until the soles of my feet wear out.
I am going to preach the gospel
That came out from His lips,
And not the words of denial

That came out of my lips…

Apostle Peter's profession while he
was preaching the gospel, after he repented
of denying the Lord and being changed by
meeting the resurrected Lord.

I sense the traces of the Lord today also

I wish I learned deep in my heart
To truly love the Lord
In serving Him…
My Lord, my Lord,
Now I am keeping Your words.
I am working for Your kingdom.

I remember Your precious words once again
And I am repenting of my foolish past.
Your touches with so much love for me,
Are now moving the depths of my heart.

Thinking of the Lord who is always with me,
And thinking of the Lord who is looking at me,
I sense the traces of the Lord during this short rest.
I hope to be at the bosom of the Lord
Just for a moment
And deliver my heart to You, Lord.

Thinking of the Lord who is with me and leading me,
I also think about the way that I have to take.

I think not only of the duty as a disciple,
But also of Your grace and love.

With such a grateful heart
I will keep on going until You call me.
Lord, my Lord, and my Father.

Apostle Peter's profession made
when he was at a place where he was with
the Lord, feeling the traces of the Lord and
making up his mind once again.

With the love the Lord has given me

Lord, because my heart waits so earnestly for You
I thought it might be You…
But it was just the sound of the breeze.

In silence of the night,
Tears roll down my face
Because of my yearning for the Lord
That floods my heart,
And because of my thoughts about the past.

I walked this way with the Lord…
I ate this with the Lord…
The Lord spoke these words to me…
As I remember each and every thing,
Everything was Your love.
Had I had the kind of heart that I have now,
I could have been more strength to You Lord…

Lord, I work with all my strength and all my heart.
With the love that You have given to me,
I powerfully march towards Your kingdom.

Apostle Peter's profession made
with his yearning for the Lord, feeling the
Lord even with the sound of breezes after a
day's work is over

If I had the heart then
that is my heart now

I remember the times
When I was going many places with the Lord.
I just loved the Lord in my own immature way.
I just loved the word and the power of the Lord,
And I was condescending as if I were the Lord.

I did not keep in mind what the Lord told me,
And I just did what I liked
And followed Him in my own way.
Every time the Lord spoke to me
I thought He was just lifting me up,
And I did not understand
The deep meaning of His words.

If I had the heart then that is the heart that I have now,
I would serve the Lord with all my heart...
My Lord, now I am coming to You.
As always, You will embrace me
In Your warm and comfortable bosom,
And now I go to Your bosom where You will hold me.

I love You, Lord!

Apostle Peter's profession offered
after he was changed into a man of spirit,
thinking of the Lord who accepted him when
he was still immature

I go to the Lord's side now

That cross
Is the glory of the Lord, who is my love,
And what an honor to be hung on that cross!
I can only give thanks
That the Lord has given me this glory.

What did the Lord think of me
When He saw me as a child?
Now, my eyes are looking at that cross,
Just like the Lord's eyes looked at His cross…
Well…

Lord,
When You were with us,
If I had the heart then that is the heart I have now,
I would have wiped out Your tears…

But You still loved me and told me many things
And let me realize.
You let me remember all this
Before my life is taken,

And You let me reminisce
And give thanks with hot tears…

Lord, I did nothing,
But I, Peter, can give my heart to the Lord,
And now I am going to see You.
I could not please You when You were with us,
But now, I will be at Your side with joy.

My long beard and silver hair
Tell me that much time has passed.
But I, Peter, have been the same all these years,
And Lord, You know this.
Now, I let go of everything peacefully
And be at Your side.

Apostle Peter's profession of joy and
thanksgiving that he made looking at the cross
on which he would be hung upside down just
before his martyrdom.

See the perfect love of the Lord

As I look back on my past days that I have lived
As I am about to see the end of my life
On this cross,

I would like to be able to convey my apologies
To my colleagues,
Those who just overlooked
My immaturity and rudeness,
But the situation will not let me.

I am going to the place
Where I can see the beloved Lord forever
Who stretched out His warm hands and led me,
And once again,
I'd like to say,

"Lord, forgive me."
"I was foolish, but now I have overcome.
And now I am going to You."
"I wanted to accomplish more things
On this earth that I am seeing now,

But I believe those who remain
Will bear many more fruits."
These are the things that I want to say.

I want to tell them
Not to break the heart of the Lord
Like I, Peter, did.
I want them to see the perfect love of the Lord.

Now, my soul sees the Lord
And will eternally take a rest.

Apostle Peter's profession offered to the Lord
and his advice he wanted to give to those who
remain when he finished his ministry and was
hung on the cross

Solving the mysteries of the Father

Thank You for giving me
A voice to cry out.

Father, among those who were loved by the Lord,
I was chosen to solve the mysteries of the Father.

My knees feel like they are breaking,
And this dark place
Is filled with the sound
Of my voice crying out.

I do not forget even for a moment
The sufferings of the Lord,
And I just give thanks
For all circumstances allowed to me
And this precious duty.

Until everyone gathers together
And talks about the accomplishing each one's ministry
And profess love before the Lord at His bosom,
I kneel down again and again

And fulfill all the works of the Father.

I am not afraid of anything,
Because the Lord and the Father are here,
And They love me.

Apostle John's profession offered while he
was crying out in prayers to receive deep
revelations during his exile to Patmos Island

In exile I am waiting for the face of the Lord

I have a duty given to me,
And as the Lord has spoken to me,
I prostrate myself in this place.

Without the guidance of the Lord,
How could I talk about
The works of the Lord
And the kingdom of the Father today?

The only wish I have
Is to be at the bosom of the Lord,
For it has been quite some time since the Lord left.

It seems that so much time has passed,
But also it feels like a moment,
As I am waiting for the face of the Lord
In this exile place.

I give thanks for that the time is coming to me
So that all will gather and see the Lord's face,
Talking with Him and remembering the past,

Just like the time when the Lord was with us.

Is it today? It is tomorrow?
I am yearning for the day to meet the Lord,
And Lord, let that day be fulfilled for me.

Apostle John's profession offered with his
longing for the day to meet the Lord at
Patmos Island, his place of exile.

As comfortable as the bosom of the Lord

Oh, how wondrous!
With the foolishness of people,
They cannot understand the providence of the Father.
How could I express this limitless heart of the Father?

Lord,
While You were here,
You showed many things,
Did many things, and spoke of many things
To let us know those many things.

There is nobody around,
But the Spirit of the Lord surrounds me,
And I feel as comfortable as in the bosom of the Lord.

Tears roll down the face
Of this old servant of the Lord,
For my yearning and longing
Cannot be expressed in any way.
My heart is still like a child
Who wants to play at the bosom of the Lord,

But the time has passed,
And I am here,
And the Lord is there…

Lord,
All these hours of my longing have been stored up
And now I am coming closer to You.

Apostle John's profession offered with thanks
and longing for the Lord reminiscing over
his past life, after fulfilling his duty even in
difficult circumstances

I will spread His love

Will there be anybody who is as foolish as I am?
I persecuted the Lord and despised His name.
I could not receive grace
For I was filled with my own thoughts,
And I insisted on my own righteousness.

And yet He warmly came to such a person as me.
I walk this way day after day
With the hope to see Him,
And to be embraced at His bosom.

Such a precious duty is given to me.
This duty is to spread the love of the Lord.
I will spread His love,
With all my heart and with my everything.

I will work with all my life until He calls me,
So that I won't be ashamed of my actions.
My beloved One, my Lord.

A profession of the apostle Paul, who at
one time persecuted believers in the Lord,
but became an apostle for the Gentiles and
worked with all his life after meeting the Lord
in the dazzling lights.

How thankful!

My Lord,
Thank You!

Even when I am beaten in the name of the Lord,
I am still thankful.

I am nothing,
But You love me so much,
That You let me receive persecution
In Your glorious name,
And I am so thankful.

I give thanks to You for giving me this grace,
Even though I am the foremost of all sinners.

A profession of thanks of the apostle Paul
offered after he received forty lashes minus
one while preaching the gospel of the Lord.

Watching the endless sea

I give thanks
For letting me think of the Lord in this place.
My feet get to rest, and my body gets a rest, too.

Watching the endless open sea,
I think of the greatness of the Father.

The billows of the Lord's endless love
For the souls flood my heart.

I am not afraid of any danger,
Because I have the Lord,
And I have my Father.

My Father, my Lord,
I love You and I thank You
For giving me praises and thanksgiving on my lips.

A profession made by the apostle Paul who
was in the sea after a shipwreck, giving thanks
even in a situation where he could not expect
to be saved

Open my way

The sky at dawn is filled with stars,
And each of the stars
Is like an eye of the Lord filled with love.
Lord, were You also watching these stars?
Were You also watching these beautiful lights
That tint the color of the sky?

What did You harbor in Your heart?
Did You miss the Father,
As I miss You?
What have You engraved in the sky?
Have You engraved my face
And let me watch the sky now?

Lord,
My heart is thoroughly and completely with You,
And I am overwhelmed by this burning heart of mine.
As it was yesterday
And as it is today
And will be tomorrow,
I still only want to testify the Lord more.

Therefore please open my way.

A profession of the Apostle Paul offered
while watching the stars in the sky just after
his ship-wreck when he was in the sea a day
and a night (2 Corinthians 11)

I praise You with my voice raised

I praise You with joy.

I lift my voice and give praises
To the One who is great
And whose name is above all names.

I give only thanks
That I have breath and I can open my mouth
And that I can praise the Lord with my mouth.

I praise the Father with all my strength
And my soul is filled and overflowing with joy.

I praise that our Father
And the Lord
Are above all these people.

I praise the great One with all my might.

Profession in the praise that
Paul and Silas offered up when they were
imprisoned while preaching the gospel

Lord, I give thanks

Lord,
I give thanks
For I can open my eyes again,
For the burning passion in my heart
To testify about the works of the Lord is not quenched,
For I can stand my body up and walk,
For I can feel the sufferings of the Lord
even for a moment.

I give thanks,
That I became an apostle who is persecuted
For the name of the Lord,
And not one who persecutes the Lord.

Profession of the apostle Paul
offered as he was going back into the city after
he was stoned and thrown out of the city.

My yearning to see the Lord

My Lord,
What matters is not whether my life is long or short.
It is not that I am hasty or impatient.
It is not that whether I will be on this earth
For many days or not.
It is just that my yearning to see You is so great.

There were many people before me,
Many people gave their lives for the Lord,
And I think that all of them had the same kind of heart
As that of mine.

I became a son of the Father,
I became a beloved son who calls on the Lord,
And I became a son
Who fulfills the duty given on this earth.

But at one corner of my heart
I always have this yearning to see the Lord,
And it brings me to tears again today
As I look up into the sky.

I am not sad for being persecuted
And going through hardships.
My tears are only for my concerns
For the works of the Father, for the souls,
And the earnest longing I have to see the Lord.

My Lord, my Father,
I look forward to the day
When these tears will stop.
I love You, my Lord!

The apostle Paul's profession
offered as he was looking up to the sky for a
moment while he was spreading the gospel
without a rest

Everything is the grace of the Lord

My sufferings
Cannot compare with those of the Lord
I am ashamed to talk about them.
And yet the warm comfort of the Lord gives me strength
And stands me up.
How can I not say all these things
Are the grace of the Lord?

I can breathe,
I can lie down,
I can speak and preach
Because it was allowed by the Lord,
And how can I not give thanks
For all these things?

Even if I have a body
I cannot testify of the Lord unless I know Him,
Even if I can walk I cannot preach
Unless I have this grace in me,
Even if I have a mouth
Every word is meaningless unless I have love.

Grace is given to me day by day.

The grace given throughout my life
Let me go the way of an apostle
And I give thanks to my Lord, the Christ
Who let me receive this honor.

I give thanks for all things;
For I can lift up my eyes and look up to the sky,
With eyes flowing with salty hot tears on my cheeks
From such precious love.

There is joy
Because my most beloved One will be there
At the end of this way that I took my whole life,
And this joy lets me endure this day.

Profession of the apostle Paul who
preached the gospel with joy and thanksgiving
even though he was being persecuted and
beaten.

If I did anything well in my life

If I did anything well in my life,
Along with the fellow workers of the Lord
It was to meet the Lord
And to accomplish the kingdom of the Father.
My body will go back to a handful of dust,
But my spirit will be in the bosom of the Lord
Whom I missed so much.

I cannot hold my tears just by thinking about it.
How much did I miss Him and yearn for Him?
Though my body is tied and cannot move,
Though my appearance is shabby,
My mind and heart feel happy and glorious
Than anybody else.

I persecuted believers for I did not know the Lord.
Some of them died because of me,
And with a desire to ask them for my forgiveness,
I always prayed thinking about them.
And with the hope
That there would be nobody like me,

I have not been lazy
In spreading the love of the Lord up
Until this moment.

As I look back, I was so happy
To preach the words of the Lord,
To manifest the power of God
And to think of the Lord at the end of the day.
My joy was so great
When the souls asked me
To teach them about the Lord.
My joy was inexplicable
When they were changed and testified about the Lord.

I do not think all these years were difficult,
Because I've always had inexpressible happiness and joy.
When I thought about the Lord,
Exhaustion or persecution did not mean anything.

Well,
My whole life was happy and joyous.

I ask myself if I could sacrifice myself more,
But what I am now,
It is precious to the Father and the Lord.

I just have something that suppresses my heart,
Which is for the souls and workers after I am gone.
But I believe that the Father has a plan
To appoint those who are proper for His kingdom
And lead them.

Those who always walked with me...
Those who always prayed for me with tears...
Those who always served me and stayed with me
For God's kingdom and for the Lord,
Their faces move my heart in this deep night.

This is only momentary separation,
And we will meet again.
Therefore I will pray for them
At the bosom of the Lord.

Father, my Father,
Lord, my beloved Lord,
Now, this son is going to the Father.

Profession of the Apostle Paul offered
before his execution, reminiscing over his life

Lord, I miss You and yearn for You exceedingly

Dear Lord!
As I think about seeing You in a very short moment,
Each of my steps towards the beheading place
Is filled with joy and thanksgiving.

My body is tied with ropes,
But my soul is free,
And I am not afraid of death at all.

As I think that I will be able to see the Lord in person,
Whom I missed and yearned for so exceedingly,
I take my steps towards the Lord with a buoyant heart.

On my way to Damascus
Lord, You came to me first
And met me in brilliant lights.

I was persecuting You,
And I caused harm before Your face,
And now You receive me in the glory,
And how can I pay back all Your grace and love?

Lord, I tried to preach the gospel with all my life,
But I look back at myself once again
As to whether I fulfilled completely
The duty that You gave me.

Lord, remember
My beloved ones who spread the gospel with me
During all these years.
Now, as I go to Your side,
I cannot stop thinking about
Those who will be left behind,
And therefore, hold them
With Your love that held me.

As I look back at my whole life,
The only word I can say to You is 'Thank You'.
You called such a little person as me,
You renewed me with Your love,
You filled my heart fully with Your love,
You led me by Your will

And manifested Your power.

I will see my beloved Lord very soon!
My heart is full and even overflowing with
The joy of meeting the Lord.
And Lord, receive my spirit!

Profession of the apostle Paul offered as he
was going towards the beheading place

You were there with me

I am just going my way, and therefore,
Do not shed your tears for me, but only for the souls.

Because you were there with me,
My ministry was strengthened,
Because you were there with me,
It was shining with lights.
This is only momentary separation,
And I hope to see all of you again with joy.

You remember my death in order to make known
How happy a death it is
When a person who loves the Lord dies,
And to show how glorious
It is to die in the name of the Lord,

And thus, in your memories,
I, Apostle Paul, should be just a person
Who went away earlier than you,
Willingly and happily giving his life for the Lord.
And I just hope

That your lives will have only the Lord and the truth.

Apostle Paul's advice given to those who were
watching him with desperate hearts when he
arrived at the place of his execution

The glory given to me is great

Lord, are You the Lord who fills my heart completely?
Are You the Lord whom I missed so much,
And called out to again and again with tears?
Because the glory You gave me is so great,
I cannot lift up my head.

Why do You give me these many things?
I have not given anything to You,
And I just worked with
What You have given me,
And I am amazed
By the greatness of the glory given to me.

Now, I lay down my duty, the duty of an apostle,
And go to Your side.
Thanks to this duty
Through which I can go to Your side,
I have been so joyous, happy, and thankful.

Now, I return to Your bosom with gladness.
Just consider those who remain,

And hold them with Your strength.
I am going to the bosom of my beloved Lord.

Profession of the apostle Paul offered seeing
the Lord who was waiting for him just before
his death at the beheading place

Advice of the Lord

Remember the tears and blood
That I shed for My beloved ones.
Think of the shepherd
Whom the Father sent at this end time.
Do not be overcome by evil and the world,
Which are nothing.

Remember those who lived in glory
Following the calling of the Father.
Do not make the price of my blood vain.

I am always close to you,
And I am watching you.
Do not cover My eyes, do not cover My heart.
I always pray
That all will participate in the resurrection.

I want you to always feel
This earnest heart of Mine through your shepherd,
I want you to always feel
The Holy Spirit who is in you.

The Lord's advice to us believers
who are living in the end time

It is My joy!

Those who make My name honorable,
Their names are shining!

Each of their names is being stored up,
And it is My joy!

The evil of the world prevails,
And it disgraces the Father's name and My name,
Yet evil is not true.
It cannot compare with the things
that will be unfolded soon.
The glory of these things will be beyond words.
Nobody will be able to match with
or stop the Father's glory.

I pray every day for them,
And the Father's will is fulfilled.

Lord's profession made with His
earnest desire for us to become true children
who are holy, and to be changed and reach a
glorious position.

Chapter 3

Father, Lord, Me

Let me know the deep will of the Father

Dear Father,
Today, as in all the other days,
I came up to this mountain
And knelt before You
To know the true will of the Father.

My beloved Father,
Had Your word not been with me,
How would I know Your will,
And how would I know
The heart of my dear Father and the Lord?
This word is my guide,
And the cord that binds You and me.

There are many believers,
But no one understands the true will of the Father,
No one can fathom the deep heart of the Father.
From Genesis to Revelation,
Let me know the deep and various will of the Father
That I may understand the secrets in the Bible
That You have hidden.

This son would only want
to spread the deep love of the Father.
I would only want many people
To believe in You truly
Without having any misunderstandings about You.

My beloved Father, my Lord,
I am on my knees on this mountain
To understand the will of the Father,
And why is it that I miss
The Father and the Lord so much?
Tears never cease to flow down from my eyes.
And, as if I were in the bosom of the Father
And the bosom of the Lord,
I would like to feel
The heart of the Father completely in this place.

Father,
My Father, whom I miss so dearly,
The yearning for You
That comes out from my heart is endless.

A profession offered at the beginning of
the church while fasting and praying on the
prayer mountain to receive understanding of
the Bible from God

For Your vision is so great

I have acted only with faith.
The heart of this servant of Yours
Was always the same
Whatever You told me to do.

As the days and time passed,
My heart only became deeper and deeper
For the Father, the Lord, and the souls.
This has become love, and power.

Just a little more, just a little more,
Let the power of the Father and the Lord
Be manifested.
Let His glory be revealed just a little more.
Let just a few more people
Know the Father and the Lord.
This is what I have been praying for.

Let them know
That my tears and hunger of my heart are for them,

I pray exerting more strength.
For Your vision is so great,
This servant is going forward
Even today without ceasing.

The great plan that You've given to me,
And to this church…
I can fulfill it. I can do it
Because of the Father
And because of my dear Lord, I can do it.

A prayer offered while marching
only with faith to reveal the glory of the Father
God and the Lord right after the opening of
the church

To keep the flock entrusted
by the Father

Nobody
Can sever the cord of my love…
My longing, my passion,
And my desperate concerns…

For I have always sought to reveal
The glory of the Father and the glory of the Lord,
And because the Father and the Lord know
This son better than anybody,
I am overcoming everything.

No matter what the people may say,
Their foolishness
Only makes me have pity on them.
So that the Father will remember
This compassion of mine,
Even today I give all my heart
For their salvation and for the flock of my dear Father.

Father…
My beloved Father…

Physically I have no strength even to open my mouth,
Yet I gather my strength in my hands
And I try to focus my mind and cry out.
I do not have the leisure
To think of my body or my situation,
While trying to keep watch over my beloved flock.

I am so desperate,
And with earnest desire
I lace my fingers with all my strength and pray
To protect the flock given by the Father.

I exert my strength,
And I try again.
I shed so many tears that I wonder
If there are any more tears left,
But they roll down my face again.
This is my heart
For the Father, the Lord, and the souls.

I remember and keep in mind again and again

That You told me this is for blessing,
As this day is going to pass by.

Father, Lord, because You are always beside me,
I gain strength and can again go on,
Because I believe it is for blessing.

I think of the way of the apostle Paul
And how severe his sufferings were,
And then I wonder
If I would be able to go the same way.
He just gave thanks even in such great hardships.
The more I think about him,
The deep impression it has made
Causes tears to flow down my face.

The way given to me has not been a way that is easy,
But if You told me to go this way again,
I would again surely be going this way.

A prayer offered during a Daniel
Prayer meeting during the trial of blessing in
1999

May the Father's will be done on this Earth

If the Father says, 'Go!',
I just go.
Let the Father's will be done on this earth.

Guarantee this son,
To reveal Your great glory.

A prayer offered to God as the
door of world evangelism opened in 2000 by
the will of God.

Though nothing was visible

The endless heart of this son for the souls
Is my earnest desire for even just one more of them
To know the Lord.
Let the gospel of the kingdom of Heaven,
The Word of life, and the power of the Father
Be manifested in full scale
For the souls going the way of death.

Though nothing was visible,
I've only marched forward up until today;
I've had only professions of faith on my lips;
I've stored up earnest prayers
Longing for the Father in my heart.
The Father has watched all these things
And guarantees this son,
And this son is able to live
Because of the comfort of the Father.

The Father lets me overcome with faith,
All those situations that seemed so very difficult,
And I take after the heart of the Father

Evermore deeply.

Let my dear workers have eyes of faith,
Let my dear workers have lips of faith,
Let my dear souls
Receive the blessings and answers of the Father…
Father, let Your glory shine to the fullest extent!

A prayer looking for the will of
God that was offered for the souls during the
flight to Uganda for a crusade in 2000.

At the Sea of Galilee

My dear Lord,
Were You here?
Where have You passed?
What did You think and what did You speak of?

This son knelt down by the command of the Father.
I do not yet know fully what the original voice is,
But, by the command of the Father
I kneel at this place
That my beloved Lord looked from
To do the will of the Father.

Has the voice of the Lord remained here
Waiting for the voice of this son?
The place that I am looking from
Is the same place that the Lord looked from,
And this touches the heart of this son.
Lord, what kind of mind did You have
When You were here?

I have many souls and their service

So that I lack nothing.
Many souls love me and follow me,
And I lack nothing.

I just knelt here
In order to fulfill the will of the Father completely.
Yet the ministry given to me cannot compare
With that of the Lord.
The Father wipes away my tears,
The Lord wipes away my tears,
And my beloved ones will wipe them away too.

I do everything only for the glory of the Father,
And therefore, Father, do not be worried.
The voice that was sounded forth today
Will shine the light for the glory of the Lord,
And this son will wait with faith.

A prayer offered during the
pilgrimage in 2004, in a place where the trace
of the Lord is felt at Galilee in preparation for
the forthcoming ministry.

With the heart of the Lord

My Father,
There are those who are cherished
In the sight of the Father,
While there are those who are not,
But to this son of Yours,
Isn't every one of them
So very precious?

Even though they are little ones,
Even though they have not cast away flesh yet,
To me all of them are my fruits,
Which I have to change beautifully
Before You Father.

And thus, even though they lack many things,
Even though they are souls who cannot be forgiven,
I mourned for them understanding their hearts,
And I prayed
So that they can be forgiven before the Father
And that they would be given another chance.

When the Lord came to this earth,
He received glory from the people,
But He also suffered
And received much contempt and maltreatment.

But the Lord loved the souls until the end,
And He understood the hearts of those souls.
He prayed that they would be given a chance
By all means possible.

As I have the same heart in my heart,
I have been running this race
With the desire not to forsake even just one soul.

Father, You know
That I have never forgotten
The Father's heart cherishing each soul,
And that I cherished all servants of the Lord
As my life
Whether they are lacking little or lacking more.

Even when there were
Those who were hiding from me,
I always prayed
That they would receive grace and strength again
And perform their duties as servants of the Lord.

Even for those servants
Who had so many fleshly thoughts
And so many incidents of disobedience,
I did not rebuke them or point out their shortcomings.
Instead, I understood
That they would suffer in themselves
Because they held so many fleshly thoughts.

My Father, You know
That I always harbored them in my heart
And prayed for them before You Father,
So that they would receive the power
To demolish their thoughts
And be able to obey.

I have never considered the mourning
And the heavy burdens for the souls to be toilsome.
But I rather considered it my joy
To do my duty of praying for them.
And I give You thanks
For giving me the power
To change them through those prayers.
Father, You heard my prayers.

Father, until I see You,
This son will change more souls
With the same mindset,
And I will pray more every day
To lead these servants whom You entrusted to me
To make them more powerful servants
And the kinds of servants whom You really want.

I will not forsake them,
But harbor them in my heart and pray for them.
And in doing so, Father,
Give them grace and change them.

Make them grow up
So that when the duty of end time
That was given to me is to be fulfilled,
They will have become a force in many areas
And be able to give glory to You, Father.

Father, in my heart,
I have no discomfort,
I do not feel even the slightest hint of hardship,
But I just believe that they will completely change.

I just believe and pray
That they will produce perfect fruits
Before You Father.

Father, remember them,
So they will be able to perform their duties as servants.
Let them be awakened
So that they won't do anything embarrassing
Before the Father.

Just as this son, in Your eyes,
Came forth with light, goodness, and truthfulness,
Let them also be the same.
Give them a chance,
Give them the Father's grace and strength,
And lead them to be able to accomplish and fulfill
Their hearts' desires and wishes.

A prayer offered with the heart of
the Lord for the servants of the Lord who are
taking care of the souls

Hear the earnest plea

Father,
Due to this son's fault, before You I show
These many embarrassing and shameful letters.

I tried with all my heart to save them,
Even by giving my life,
But today, before You I show these many shames.

But Father,
I confess
That You always guided this son and this church
With only good things.

Father,
Hear my heart-rending prayers
To save these souls, and open the way.
Show them the light and allow for them to receive salvation.

I have always been faithful before You, Father,
And I have always sought good things before You.
Father, Abba Father!

Show Your mercy
And show Your good will
To numerous souls of this church.

My life, and my everything
Has always belonged to You, Father.

No matter what is required of me,
No matter what You asked me to give,
Everything is Yours, and I do not spare anything.
But one thing I cherish
Is the love that You gave for these souls.
Let this love be revealed in perfection.

Prayer of the shepherd who is
earnestly praying before God for the souls
who committed sins in disobedience to the
Word of God.

Open the way to save them

Father, my Father,
You say it is not true,
But no matter how much I think,
It is my fault that I did not teach them right.

Just a little harder,
If I had taught them the truth just a little harder,
Today, I wouldn't have been so ashamed
Before You, Father.

What can I say about those souls?
I am responsible, and I am their shepherd...

I cannot just quit or resign
Saying I want to assume the responsibility myself,
Because I know that I have to achieve what the Father wants
Taking the responsibility for all these things.
And it is for this reason, Father, on my knees
This son asks You for forgiveness.
I will take any measure,
If it can save them,

And thus, Father open a way…
Open a way to save them.

Because only You, Father
Can do it,
This son dares to confess their sins,
And asks You, Father, for forgiveness.

Father, help them.
Save them!

Prayer offered on the Christmas
of 2010 with a burning heart asking God to
open a way for salvation for those members
of church who had committed sins.

Longing for the day to give glory

Thank You! My dear Father!
It's been almost 30 years since You gave me this duty.
I have been glorifying You through many things,
And I have prayed and fasted,
But I only feel ashamed looking back on the past.

Sparing nothing and saving all my time
I gave everything to You,
With my love for You and with my love for the souls
I tried only to give glory to You, Father.
But I only feel embarrassed
If I think about what was achieved.

Abba Father, in these many busy days,
There were many things to harbor and to accomplish,
And I tried to be diligent in all matters,
Yet Father, as You recall, let me know.

Let me know whether or not
This son was lazy before You,
As I look back again, let me know

Whether or not I paid full attention in all things.
Dear Father, I ask You for the perfect sanctuary
To offer up to You,
And I ask You for men of spirit
With whom You would be pleased.

I am longing for the day when the faces and hearts
Of those whom I love will be engraved
In You, Father, and give You glory.
I thank You
For letting this son's tearful prayers,
Petitions, and mournful supplications
Be borne as the fruit of answers and blessings.

Still I desire that more souls
Will come forth as hearts of spirit.
Father, give them great grace
So that they can cast away sins
And the worldly things completely
And live only for You, Father.

Until the Lord comes back,
This son will not give up on any of these souls.
I will lead even just one more soul into the place.
Father, add grace upon grace.

Prayer offered to the Father God
just before the 30th anniversary of the church,
with the love for the souls, not giving up on
any of them

You consider these tears priceless

Father,
I give You thanks.

Your good will was with this church,
And it let the souls grow up to be as they are now.
I give You thanks.

You considered the tears of this son
To be priceless and accepted them,
And today You have given me this joy.

Father, I give You thanks.

Prayer offered to the Father
God with thanks for the believers who
have departed from sin, who are cultivating
holiness, and who are changing into men of
spirit and whole spirit

While I have my breath

Father, 10 years ago, 20 years ago, and 30 years ago
I prayed with the same consistent heart.
As the person who was put in charge of this church,
My heart has been consistent before You Father.

Even though I could not see anything,
I only thought of the blessing
And glory of the Father at the end.
While I have my breath,
I have thought only of the Father, the Lord,
And the souls.

Even as my sight was dimmed
And my ears were deafened,
I only thought about the will of the Father in it.
I only desire to give fullness of the Spirit,
Joy, and happiness
To these beloved ones whom I am leading.

My beloved Father,
Today and tomorrow this son will go on

Thinking only about the great and grand things
That You have prepared.
Father, let Your will be done.

Prayer offered thinking only about
the will of the Father God and the souls for
more than 30 years of pastoral ministry

His deep love for the souls

Father,
You are truly beautiful and perfect.
How can this son express Your depth and width?
Your patience and Your endurance are limitless.

This son desires to let all the souls of this earth know
About the Father's providence in human cultivation
And Your deep love for the souls,
Which is my duty that nobody else can fulfill.

How many tears have You shed for the poor souls,
And how much have You sacrificed?

Beloved Father,
Yesterday, today, and tomorrow,
This son thinks and will think of the Father's heart
And the things that You will accomplish.

I hope that this burning love of mine for the souls
Is sufficient to cover so many souls.

Prayer containing the desire to spread the
deep love of the Father God to all peoples

Offering up the festival of blessing

Father, have You come?
I feel You, but I cannot see Your face
That I really want to see.
And Father, do You feel
This desperate heart of this son?

I want to pour out all the earnestness
That is in my heart,
While resting at Your bosom.
Yet, by my eyes my beloved Father is not yet seen,
And my earnest heart only becomes
More earnest and desperate.

Father, as You have come and seen,
As You have laid Your eyes upon this church,
Everything is what You have done.
Accept the heart of this son
Who wants to offer everything to You
In greater perfection.
If You, Father, do not help me,
You know that this son is nothing.

Father, greatly and even more greatly,
May this son's desperate heart be accomplished
As blessings for this earth.

Today too I exert all my strength

To feel the limitations of this earth,
It is not something easy.
My Lord... Was Your ministry on this earth similar?

Great power was given to me,
But sometimes it is unbearable sorrow for me,
That things can only be done
When the measure of justice
Is fulfilled in the Father's will.

But I can overcome today and also tomorrow,
Because I love the Father,
And because so many souls are together with me.
Therefore, I will not stop.

Today, tomorrow and every day,
I will exert all my heart, all my will,
And all my strength
To let the will of the Father alone be done.

I still have the strength to breathe

And my heart is burning and passionate
For the Father, for the Father's kingdom,
And for the souls.
For this reason I take on all the burdens
And assume all the duties.

My beloved Father,
My beloved Father, my beloved Lord,
I exert all my strength even today
For the flock of the Father, that I love.

A profession offered up desiring to
march on with full strength until the power of
God is perfectly manifested

To ride on the flow of spirit
and march on vigorously

The providence of the Father God
Has always been great.
It is so grand that it gives me strength,
And it leads the children of the Father,
Through the things that the Father
Has shown and manifested.
Father I thank You!

Always Father, You did it.
Always Father, You gave.
Always Father, You showed.
That is why today so many of these souls
Are marching on
And vigorously riding
On the flow of spirit of the Father.

I want this blessing of the Father
To be given not just to certain people,
But to all peoples.
I do not want anybody to fall behind.

I want everyone to participate in this flow
To depart from sins and evil
And to live in the love of the Father.
This son knows very well
This is the will of the Father.
I want everyone to hold onto
This chance of grace You've given.

Prayer offered up to the Father God hoping
all the believers to ride on the flow of spirit
and change into true children of God

There is no one to whom my love does not reach out

My Father, my Father,
It is by Your grace that I can stand.
It is also by Your grace
That I can be with the flock
That You have entrusted to me.

My dear Father,
This son has a desire in his heart,
And I offer it up to You with all my heart.

I want all those who belong to me
To ride on this flow of spirit more perfectly
And I want to quickly accomplish this vision
You have given me.

Some of the flock have been with me for 30 years,
Others for 20 years and still others for 10 years.
Some shed tears with me in difficult times,
While others were foolish
And sought their own benefit.
But, all of them are the flock of this son.

Since I desired that not one of them
Fall away from this fold,
Father, You allowed for me
To sound forth the original voice.

Father, You know
That I do not want to forsake anybody,
And there is no one
To whom my love does not reach out.

Due to lack of strength my sight is dimmed,
And my legs are without strength,
But I still try to pull myself together.

And yet my heart is joyful
Considering Your promise, Father.
I believe it is a blessing for them.
So, I gather my senses
And deliver the will of the Father.

I'd like my heart

To be delivered deeply to them,
To these beloved souls.

Prayer offered just before the New Year
service for 2013, wishing that not a single soul
should fall behind.

Taking my steps to the mountains

Father,
Now again, according to Your command,
I move with my steps toward the mountains.

The original voice was sounded forth
For my beloved souls,
So let the complete fullness of the voice
Come upon them
Without any part of it gone missing.

This son has always obeyed You alone, Father,
And You know the heart of this son.
Let the strength to pray and the power to change
Fully come upon these beloved souls of mine.

I did all my best today with all my strength
Working for the Father and the souls.
And therefore, Father,
Achieve all these things within Your perfection,
And I commit all these beloved souls into Your hands.

Prayer offered to the Father God committing
the beloved souls into His hands after the
New Year service for 2013.

How can I let them live?

Father,
Today also, this son sees the sins of these souls.

They misunderstood You for they were foolish.
And they are in agony
Because they misunderstood the Lord and this son,
And this breaks my heart.

How can they think such things?
No matter how many times I ask myself,
I can only ask You, Father, to forgive them.

I do not hate them or dislike them,
But rather I feel pitiful,
And I only think of ways to let them live.

Father, was it so for You, too?
Dear Lord, was it the same for You, too?
Have You endured such a long, long time,
Waiting for the souls and enduring with them?
I can thoroughly feel deep in my heart,

The love of the Father, the love of the Lord,
And the depth of Your hearts.

Until the end, until the Lord comes back,
This son will not give up on them.

I will endure and bear with them and lead them,
Until these souls You, Father, created will change
And change completely.

For this duty given by You, Father,
For this precious duty, I willingly take
Today's tears, and tomorrow's tears.

Prayer offered with tears and burning heart
during the mountain prayer in 2013 for the
church members who were suffering in the
swamps of sins

The Father's heart

Father, I know Your heart.
This son knows the love of the Father
Who wants to save them.

The origin of the Father is love,
And Your heart is to let them live.

You speak as though You are very angry at them,
But I know that in Your heart,
You have the tears for them.

Father, You always give me good things,
And You always give me only comfort,
And how can I say I do not know Your heart?

They also know Your endurance, Father,
And this event today let them understand deeply
The heart of the Father again.

Thank You,
I love You.

My Father,
I want to be at Your bosom
That is so wide and beautiful,
But I will wait.
Until You call me…

Prayer of the shepherd offered while he was
receiving the spiritual sword of punishment
that is given by God to those souls who had
committed grave sins that would deprive them
of salvation

For the glory of the Father
which is at the end of this waiting

On my eyes, my ears, my head, and my body…
Even though the fact that I cannot do anything
As I want tortures me,
My heart is still completely filled with love
That enables me to do anything.

I overcome this moment solely
With the power of that love.
This hardship cannot be endured
Even with faith or hope,
And I am enduring it only with love.

When I lie down or sit,
Or even when I do not even know
That I am holding a spoon in my hand,
Even when I cannot feel myself
As to whether I am standing or not,
I am looking up to the Father, only the Father
So desperately and earnestly.

I forget that I am a person,

That I have a body, that it's evening now,
Or it's the time for the dear believers to gather.
For the last 31 years, my heart has never left
My beloved church members,
The flock of the Father…
It is sad and tormenting
That I cannot sense with my own will
The time they gather
And the time they offer worship service.
But my heart is filled with love,
More love than any other time.

Father,
Is my sight dim because I shed too many tears?
Are my ears dull
Because I heard so many things
That couldn't be contained?
But this is the least of my concerns.

My love and the fact that souls are changing
Stand me up, and I gather my strength again,

For the glory of the Father which is at the end of this waiting.

Profession offered during mountain prayers
while filling up the measure of justice for the
change, spiritual growth, and blessings of the
beloved church members.

I just want to let them live…

The people are foolish,
And they disgrace the Father and this son.

But Father, I do not dislike them,
But I just want to let them live,
And I just want to open a way for them to be changed.

As the Father
Let the lives of the many patriarchs
And the life of my dear Lord
Be the way of life, the way of faith,
And the way of glory always,
This son also just wants to save them…

If I think, 'Until when? How much more?
And I can no longer…'
It seems they have done too much,
But my heart still loves them,
And I again just want to let them live.

Father,

Let Your justice
Turn into Your love,
And Father, let Your will be done.

This son will take everything.

Prayer offered to the Father God on the
Easter of 2013, with the desire to save even
those who were disgracing God

I will comfort the Father

Father,
Did You think about me?
I try my best today,
With the grace given by You, Father.

It seems I will collapse
If I loosen up for a moment,
But I feel the strength
That You are giving me,
And I collect my mind and do Your will.

Thinking of the past days
That I spent with so many tears,
How could this son endure,
If it weren't for the Father's grace?

But how could my agony
Compare with the agony of the Father?
You think about my agony
And give me this grace today,
And it is Father's love.

Now, this son and this church
Will comfort the Father.
And therefore, Father,
Please stop those precious tears of Yours.

What I have now is shortness of breath, shaky legs,
And eroded eyes due to tears,
But as You said, Father,
I will come forth in resurrection.

Let the Father's providence,
The great heart of the Father
Fill this church fully.

Profession offered on the Easter of 2013,
looking forward to comforting God as the
church members would come forth in
spiritual resurrection

I did not spare anything

Father, my Father,
Not once did I ever say that
I did not like this way I've taken,
I have never regretted it.

Only if I could,
I have given and given again to these souls
My eyes, my ears, my hands, my arms,
And even my breath.
I did not spare anything to fulfill the Father's will
And to allow for the poor souls
A way that they could live.

I did not have at all such thoughts as:
'A little rest, a little slumber,
And a little bit of me and mine'.
I never insisted upon my things or my own,
And only if I could, I was not afraid,
Even if I was to be destitute or die.

This is my heart,

And this is my love for the souls of the Father.

I have thought this is the natural course of things
And how things should be.
This is how I have lived my life.

Even now, this son is thinking about
What I can give to them,
How I can give them fullness of Spirit,
And how I can give them the Father's love.

My beloved Father, my Lord,
Just by saying the Father's name on my lips
I am dying to see you,
But if not seeing You,
Although I want to see You so much,
Can give more benefit to these souls,
Then it too I give up.

My beloved Father, my Lord,
As was yesterday, today, and tomorrow as well,

I will march on with thanksgiving, love, and faith.

Profession of the shepherd made on the
Feast of Harvest in 2013, before he went up
to mountain prayers, desiring to give and give
again to the souls

Beloved church

Again as always
I have been seeking the good will of the Father
For the last thirty years,
And now, before we knew it
Those many years have already passed,
And I am here at this moment.
Now the heart of this son
Resembles the heart of the Father,
And it has been broadened
As much as the time that has passed.

Sometimes I think about
Whether I lacked anything
In giving glory to the Father,
Other times I think about
Whether I cared enough or not
Whether I could have given more to the Father,
And still at other times, I think about
Whether there is a way to let those souls live,
Even though they are like Judas Iscariot.

My heart yearns for the Father so much,
And tears upon tears well up
Because I cannot see You.
But You've remembered all those years
During which I just marched on
Looking forward to the day I will see You.
And in this church,
You have manifested such great works!

Until the day I rest at Your bosom,
This son will never stop at all,
For this son is Yours, Father.

You have rewarded all those days
During which You did not allow any rest for me
And You let Your glory alone
Be in this church.

Profession offered while looking back at
the pastoral ministry for the last 30 years
and thinking about the power of God, His
providence, and the fruit of it with faith

Trace of love

The word 'endurance'
The word 'patience',
Are these necessary words for me?

The days during which
I counted a day and then another day
And a month and then another month
And a year and then another year,
They have been stored up in my body
As traces of my love for the souls.

If only I could save them
By giving my eyes, ears, my hands and feet,
Even my organs and cells,
And if only they could go
To better heavenly dwelling places...
These are reasons why I live each day,
And I have lived these many, many days.

And the only thing that remains in me
Is the evidence of my love for them.

Even though I cannot hold my body up as I want,
I am only thankful
That, through me, many souls receive salvation,
And many souls are becoming
True children of the Father.
This is the amazing love of the Father,
And it comforts me and consoles me for the moment.

For this reason each day of my life
Is filled with only love and tears.

There is One who remembers these days,
And He is my Father;
He is my beloved Father.

Profession of the shepherd spending each
day with tears of love, looking forward to
numerous believers becoming fruits of faith

Tears of the shepherd

Father,
My Father…

I follow Your orders,
But still I do not dare to run against You yet face-to-face,
My Father, my beloved Father

You are telling me to do it,
But knowing the goodness and love of the Father,
How dare I approach the light of the Father
With that of mine?

The only thing I can do, Father,
Is to come close to You with my love;
Father, this is the attitude of my heart.

Father,
If You were in front of me now,
My heart would become flowing tears.
This is my love
And my yearning for You, Father.

Father,
I want to be embraced in Your bosom,
And I want to see You.
I want to put my heart into Your heart,
Being in Your bosom.

Even though I try to stop thinking,
Once I begin to think about You, Father,
It does not stop.
Let this heart of mine become glory to You,
Let it be the glory of the Father.

Profession of the shepherd containing
yearning love for the dear Father God

For the glory of the Father

Had I thought based on only the things I could see,
Would I have been able to understand
The heart of the Father?
Had I tried to do the things
That I wanted giving excuses to the Father,
What would have happened?

I never did such a thing,
But this little difficulty in my heart
Makes me look into little things one by one.
My heart has been only for the Father and the Lord
At every moment,
And I was thankful for it.
And I was thankful for the fact
That I did not have any self-centered desires.
But now, the Father is telling me not to rely on Him.
But yet He is my everything.

I lived all my life,
Relying on the Father and the Lord.
But the Father is telling me

To listen to the voice of the Holy Spirit in me.
I am happy
When the Father teaches me everything in detail,
And it was so easy to follow His instructions
All the time.
But, the Father is now telling me to decide
Whether to go or stop at my own discretion,
And it is about such difficult things to decide.
And yet I am thankful
Because He commands me
For He believes in me and that I can do it.
But how can I express this feeling
Of not knowing what to do?
I wonder if the Father was also
In this kind of void and vacantness.

Today, thinking about the heart of the Father,
I look back at the things that I am doing,
As to whether what I am doing is close
Enough to the Father's will.
Even though nothing is visible,

I know that the Father is my Father.
He commands me only of good things all the time,
For I've always seen the final result
Was that of goodness.

Today, I exert my strength
For my beloved ones,
And for the love of the Father,
And the glory of the Father.

Profession offered in prayers to understand
the will of God given, preparing for the end
time in God's providence

Receive the glory

Father, I have come out here
To glorify Your name.
I have only sought the glory of the Father
Day after day and year after year.

I have come to this place
Along with the beloved believers,
In order to reveal the glory of the Father.
I am happy. I am thankful.
Great will be the glory of the Father,
And I am happy.

I know what You will command of me.
Thank You.
You always move my heart.
You never miss anything that is in my heart.
Receive this glory today.

Prayer offered to the Father God
who will receive glory through amazing works
of power on the first day of the summer
retreat 2013.

Endless glory that will be revealed in the name of Manmin

Each and every day
Has been stored up through the love of the Father.
The blessing given by the Father is so great,
And blessings have been piled up
To accomplish the ministry of the Father.

I spend this day,
Looking forward to the tremendous blessings
That will be given to this church
And not just what is visible right now.

The love of the Father has changed
These beloved souls,
And it will also reach those who will be changed.
The power of the Father will be limitless.

Dear Father,
I have great expectations
Because You will show
The greatness of the power of Your love
To Manmin and all the souls,

And I look forward to the endless glory
That will be revealed in the name of Manmin...

Profession offered during the mountain prayer
to accomplish the ministry of the Father at
the end time, looking forward to the endless
blessings and glory that will be revealed

The running of my race is never ending

This is the most important moment
In my whole pastoral ministry.
The outline is being revealed
By the Father's plan,
The preparations for the evangelism of the world
With the holiness gospel.

Each of my beloved members
Who are running towards spirit and whole spirit
Prove that they are answers to my prayers.
And therefore, I believe
The providence of the end time given to me is grand.

My tears have formed a river
Proving the expression, 'a river of tears' is true.
My body is showing
That I am giving everything with the heart of parents,
And I do not spare anything.

After giving everything again and again,
All I have left is my breath.

But I leave this breath with me,
Because I have to be here,
Because there are days
When I have to be with them.
This is not a desire for myself,
But it is the most precious thing for these souls
And for the kingdom of the Father.
Therefore, even today,
I think of the souls because I have this breath,
And my running will not end
To bring forward the time of the Father.

Even though I have so many souls
Whom I want to see,
Even though many have disappeared
From my memory,
My heart will still remember everybody.

I think of each soul and each worker,
As to how they were led to this church,
What kind of faith they have,

What their prayers are,
And what kind of grace I should give to them.
I prepare to meet with my beloved ones
Not with the form that is reflected
In this physical space,
But with the love that fully fills my heart.

Profession offered after finishing the
mountain prayer just before Christmas in
2013, preparing himself to accomplish the
ministry for the end time

Until the fruit is completely ripe

As it has been said,
"I've become what I am by the grace of God,"
I wish all those belonging to me
Will not forget this grace of the Father
Given to them…
I wish they will not forget
That today could not be given
If not for the grace of the Father
In each of their lives…

Just as I was able to become their shepherd
Because I did not forget
The times of grace given to me,
I wish that my beloved ones will not forget
That the grace they are enjoying
Is actually the tears of the Father.

I wish for them not to forget the tears I shed
To lead even just one more of them
To the beautiful, truly beautiful place…

I never cared for my own interests.
Since the moment I became a shepherd,
Even when I eat, when I pray, when I breathe,
My eyes are filled with the souls.
I have never forgotten their prayer points,
The grace I have to give to them,
And the burdens that I have to carry...

But I have always been thankful,
Because I love them,
And because I love the Father...

Until my love that is embedded in each passing day
Is delivered to my beloved ones
And the fruit of that love is completely ripe,
I just go on without ceasing.

Because my love has no end,
And the Father's love has no end...

Profession with the love for the souls given
with the heart of the Father God who wants
to give only the best

The souls in the eyes of the Father

I think about the heart of the Father
Until the measure of faith,
Which they could not get on their own,
Is given to them.

I think about the love and hard-work of the Father.
Father, it was same for You;
You never said it was hard or You disliked them.

You believed them just as You believed me,
You loved them just as You loved me.

I cherished them
And wanted to lead them
To the castle of the shepherd in New Jerusalem,
And Father, You agreed.

Although they are lacking now,
Father, You look forward to the future,
And thus, I'd like for many more souls
To be fully in Your eyes.

Profession offered up to the Father God with
the hope for numerous believers to go into
the city of New Jerusalem

My beloved Father

I give thanks to You, Father,
For Your glory is revealed,
And Your perfectness is revealed.

My Father, You waited for countless days.
I give You thanks with everything I have.
You have always been with this son
And with this church.

Your glory is revealed to all the earth,
And what can I offer up this thanks with?
This son's thankfulness now becomes tears.
Father, Your endurance has become the fruit.
Now, there is peace in the heart of this son.

My Father, my beloved Father,
Today, I miss You even more,
And I cannot hold my love for You.
My dear Father, I give You thanks,
I give You thanks.

Profession that will be offered up to the
beloved Father after the construction of
Canaan Sanctuary which will be a place of
true rest

211

Profession at the Wedding Banquet in the air

Beloved Father, my Lord,
My heart is moved and filled
With inexpressible emotions,
For I can give my love for the Father to the fullest
Being in the bosom of the Father.

I wanted to see You so much.
My heart missed You and yearned for You so.
This heart became my tears,
And they wet my collar again and again.

What should I say first,
And what should I mention later?
My love and my yearning for Heaven and the Father
That I had at each moment
Let me dwell in this glory that I have now.

Father,
Besides this great joy and the overwhelming emotions,
Hear this concern I have.
Remember Your ministers

That are left on the earth,
And remember the souls
That will struggle for salvation.

In the grace and chance You will give,
Father, help those who can be saved,
Certainly to receive salvation.

Until all will partake in the banquet
That You will throw in Your plan,
Remember them deep in Your heart, Father.

My tears, all these tears
Flow down and again with the joy
And emotions of meeting You, my Father,
But also my tears of pity for those souls
Do not end either.

My Beloved Father, I love You.

Profession of the shepherd that is offered for
the first time at the bosom of the Father at the
Wedding Banquet given by the Father God
after the Lord's coming in the air.

Profession offered in New Jerusalem

My Father,
I give the souls that are shining
Like the stars and the sun in Your bosom.
The days that I spent asking and mourning
Before the Father
To bring many souls to this place
And to let them come into this beautiful place
Finally became the fruit of the Father's cultivation.

There is nothing this son has done.
All these things were achieved
Thanks to the grace of the Father
And Your perfect love.
Now, the tears of this son have become the pearl
And gained these fruits,
And I have come before the Father
Whom I missed with tears,
And therefore, I am at the warm bosom of the Father.

I wanted to see You so much.
I wanted to see You, Father,

And the Lord so much.
Wipe away all these tears of yearning
That filled my heart all these years
With Your gentle and soft hands.
My Father, my Lord!

Profession offered to the Father God after
fulfilling the providence of God at the end
time and going in the city of New Jerusalem,
the most beautiful heavenly dwelling place

Father, Lord, me

Father, Lord, me.
The names that I miss so much.
No matter how much I call them,
I miss them endlessly.

I love my Father,
My Lord,
So deeply in my heart,
Even to the extent that my heart is hurting.
They are my everything.

The love of God who in the heavenly house
engraved this profession offered on this earth,
holding the unbearable yearning to fulfill the
providence of the end time to save all peoples

The Author
Dr. Jaerock Lee

Dr. Jaerock Lee was born in Muan, Jeonnam Province, Republic of Korea, in 1943. While in his twenties, Dr. Lee suffered from a variety of incurable diseases for seven years and awaited death with no hope for recovery. However one day in the spring of 1974 he was led to a church by his sister and when he knelt down to pray, the living God immediately healed him of all his diseases.

From the moment he met the living God through that wonderful experience, Dr. Lee has loved God with all his heart and sincerity, and in 1978 he was called to be a servant of God. He prayed fervently with countless fasting prayers so that he could clearly understand the will of God, wholly accomplish it and obey the Word of God. In 1982, he founded Manmin Central Church in Seoul, Korea, and countless works of God, including miraculous healings, signs and wonders, have been taking place at his church ever since.

In 1986, Dr. Lee was ordained as a pastor at the Annual Assembly of Jesus' Sungkyul Church of Korea, and four years later in 1990, his sermons began to be broadcast in Australia, Russia, and the Philippines. Within a short time many more countries were being reached through the Far East Broadcasting Company, the Asia Broadcast Station, and the Washington Christian Radio System.

Three years later, in 1993, Manmin Central Church was selected as one of the "World's Top 50 Churches" by the *Christian World* magazine (US) and he received an Honorary Doctorate of Divinity from Christian Faith College, Florida, USA, and in 1996 he received his Ph. D. in Ministry from Kingsway Theological Seminary, Iowa, USA.

Since 1993, Dr. Lee has been spearheading world evangelization through many overseas crusades in Tanzania, Argentina, L.A., Baltimore City, Hawaii, and New York City of the USA, Uganda, Japan, Pakistan, Kenya, the Philippines, Honduras, India, Russia, Germany, Peru, Democratic Republic of the Congo, Israel and Estonia.

In 2002 he was acknowledged as a "worldwide revivalist" for his powerful ministries in various overseas crusades by major Christian newspapers in

Korea. In particular was his 'New York Crusade 2006' held in Madison Square Garden, the most famous arena in the world. The event was broadcast to 220 nations, and in his 'Israel United Crusade 2009', held at the International Convention Center (ICC) in Jerusalem he boldly proclaimed Jesus Christ is the Messiah and Savior.

His sermons are broadcast to 176 nations via satellites including GCN TV and he was listed as one of the 'Top 10 Most Influential Christian Leaders' of 2009 and 2010 by the popular Russian Christian magazine *In Victory* and news agency *Christian Telegraph* for his powerful TV broadcasting ministry and overseas church-pastoring ministry.

As of February of 2015, Manmin Central Church has a congregation of more than 120,000 members. There are 10,000 branch churches worldwide including 56 domestic branch churches, and more than 123 missionaries have been commissioned to 23 countries, including the United States, Russia, Germany, Canada, Japan, China, France, India, Kenya, and many more so far.

As of the date of this publishing, Dr. Lee has written 94 books, including bestsellers *Tasting Eternal Life before Death, My Life My Faith I & II, The Message of the Cross, The Measure of Faith, Heaven I & II, Hell, Awaken Israel!,* and *The Power of God.* His works have been translated into more than 76 languages.

His Christian columns appear on *The Hankook Ilbo, The JoongAng Daily, The Chosun Ilbo, The Dong-A Ilbo, The Munhwa Ilbo, The Seoul Shinmun, The Kyunghyang Shinmun, The Korea Economic Daily, The Korea Herald, The Shisa News,* and *The Christian Press.*

Dr. Lee is currently leader of many missionary organizations and associations. Positions include: Chairman, The United Holiness Church of Jesus Christ; President, Manmin World Mission; Permanent President, The World Christianity Revival Mission Association; Founder & Board Chairman, Global Christian Network (GCN); Founder & Board Chairman, World Christian Doctors Network (WCDN); and Founder & Board Chairman, Manmin International Seminary (MIS).

Heaven I & II

A detailed sketch of the gorgeous living environment the heavenly citizens enjoy and beautiful description of different levels of heavenly kingdoms.

The Message of the Cross

A powerful awakening message for all the people who are spiritually asleep! In this book you will find the reason Jesus is the only Savior and the true love of God.

Hell

An earnest message to all mankind from God, who wishes not even one soul to fall into the depths of hell! You will discover the never-before-revealed account of the cruel reality of the Lower Grave and Hell.

My Life My Faith I & II

Dr. Jaerock Lee's autobiography provides the most fragrant spiritual aroma for the readers, through his life extracted from the love of God blossomed in midst of the dark waves, cold yoke and the deepest despair.

The Measure of Faith

What kind of a dwelling place, crown and reward are prepared for you in heaven? This book provides with wisdom and guidance for you to measure your faith and cultivate the best and most mature faith.

Spirit, Soul, and Body I & II

A guidebook that gives the reader spiritual understanding of spirit, soul, and body, and helps him find what kind of 'self' he has made so that he can gain the power to defeat darkness and become a person of spirit.

Awaken, Israel

Why has God kept His eyes on Israel from the beginning of the world to this day? What kind of His providence has been prepared for Israel in the last days, who await the Messiah?

Seven Churches

The letter to the seven churches of the Lord in the book of Revelation is for all the churches that have existed up until now. It is like a signpost for them and a summary of all the words of God in both Old and New Testaments.

Footsteps of the Lord I & II

An unraveled account of secrets about the beginning of time, the origin of Jesus, and God's providence and love for allowing His only begotten Son Passion and resurrection!

The Power of God

A must-read that serves as an essential guide by which one can possess true faith and experience the wondrous power of God